Introduction

The Essentials of GCSE Art and Design is suitable for students working to any of the major specifications (AQA, Edexcel, OCR and WJEC/CBAC) for the full or short GCSE Art and Design course.

The specifications issued by the exam boards cover a broad subject area in very general terms. As such, they can appear vague and confusing. Written by Nick Eggleton, a Principal Examiner, Assistant Principal Moderator and working teacher, this guide has been developed to help students understand exactly what is expected of them on the course and assist them in producing coursework of the highest possible standard.

The book is divided into three main sections. The first looks at how the course is assessed and the criteria for assessment. It then goes on to explore the core elements of the course, which are relevant to all students regardless of the discipline (or endorsement) they choose to work in.

Candidates taking the full course* must choose to follow one of six course options, on the successful completion of which they will be awarded a qualification in GCSE Art and Design. The second section of the guide looks at each of these options in turn, clarifying what is required of the student. It highlights the skills, processes and considerations specific to each course option and explores the different disciplines they encompass.

*Please note that the short course is only available as the 'unendorsed' course option (i.e. students cannot choose to specialise).

The final section offers guidance on how to approach new projects and structure coursework. It breaks the process down into clear, logical stages, to assist students in developing and communicating their ideas from an initial concept through to the production and evaluation of a final piece. It covers everything that a candidate needs to include to produce a strong unit of work and achieve their full potential.

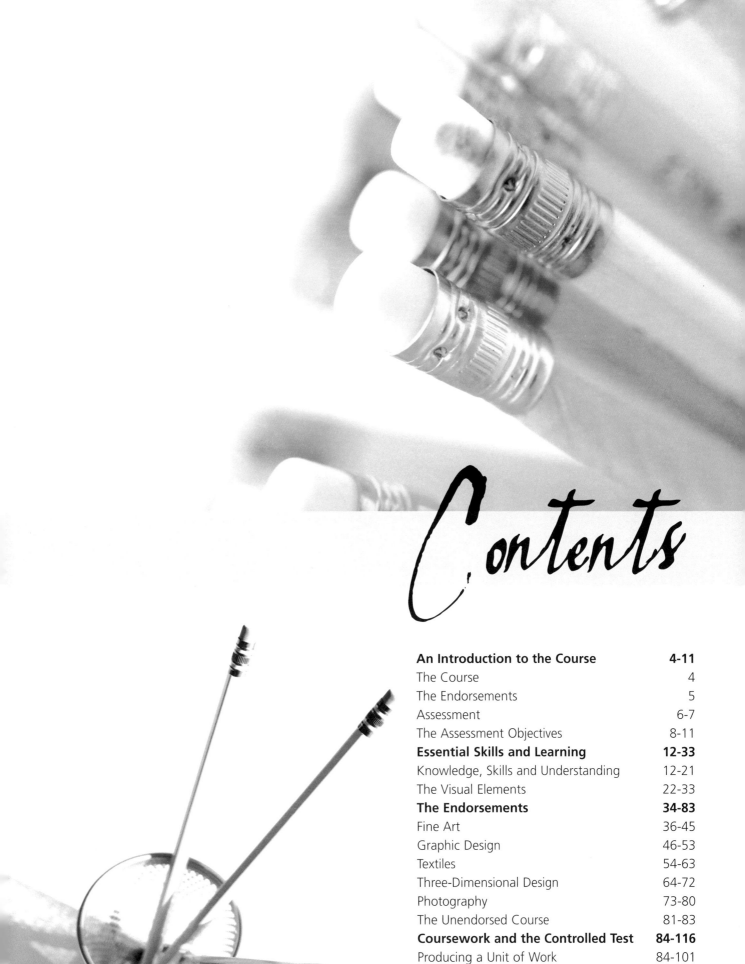

Contents

The Course

The GCSE Art and Design course focuses on three main areas: knowledge, skills and understanding. It combines the academic study of art, craft and design with creative activities and the development of practical skills.

The purpose of the theory work is to help you gain a sound knowledge and understanding of art and design practices, both past and present. You will be looking closely at pieces produced by other artists, exploring different styles and genres and investigating a whole range of materials, techniques and processes.

When it comes to producing your own work, you will then be able to draw upon what you have learned through this research and investigation. It should provide you with inspiration, help you to make informed choices and encourage you to explore avenues you might not have considered before, as you work towards a final piece.

Art and Design is a vast topic, so it is broken down into five 'endorsements' or specialist subject areas. When you begin the course you will need to choose which area you would like to work and be assessed in.

Working within a specific endorsement is a good idea if you have talents or interests that lie in one particular area. However, many students have a broad base of skills and varied interests. The 'unendorsed' course option caters for students who would like to combine two or more of the specialist subjects.

The different endorsements are shown on the facing page.

The Endorsements

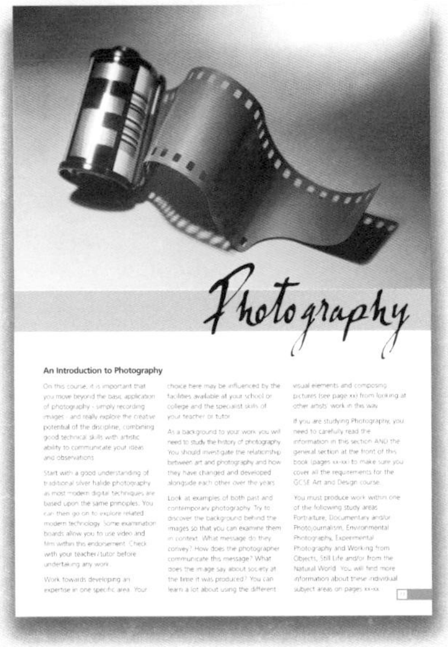

There are five endorsed study options, each of which covers a range of different themes...

Fine Art

- Drawing and/or Painting
- Sculpture, Land Art or Installation
- Printmaking
- Film or Video
- Mixed Media

Graphic Design

- Computer-Aided Design
- Illustration
- Advertising and/or Packaging
- Digital Imaging, Film, Video and/or Animation

Textiles

- Printed and/or Dyed Materials
- Domestic Textiles
- Constructed and/or Applied Textiles
- Fashion and/or Costume

Three-Dimensional Design

- Ceramics
- Sculpture
- Theatre, Television, Film and/or Exhibition Design
- Jewellery
- Interior, Product and/or Environmental Design

Photography

- Portraiture, Documentary and Photo-Journalism
- Environmental Photography
- Experimental Photography
- Working from Objects, Still Life and/or the Natural World

...and one unendorsed option, where you can combine two or more of the options shown.

Unendorsed

- Fine Art
- Graphic Design
- Textiles
- Three-Dimensional Design
- Photography

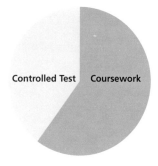

The GCSE Art and Design course is assessed on two separate components...

- **Coursework**
  60% of total marks (No time limit)
- **Controlled Test**
  40% of total marks (Time limit of 10 hours)

Coursework

Coursework refers to all the work you produce during the course, which usually lasts for 2 years. You will be expected to produce two, three or four complete 'units' of work, depending upon your examination board (if you are not sure, check with your teacher/tutor).

A single 'unit' is a package of work based around a specific theme or idea. It is made up of preparatory work, sketchbooks, logbooks, journals or technical notebooks and a final piece. Most students' preparatory work etc. is presented for assessment on mounted boards alongside the final piece; the outcome of all your research, thoughts and ideas.

There are four main objectives on which all your work will be assessed. These are looked at individually on pages 8-11. The production of coursework is looked at in greater detail on pages 84-101.

▼ An example of a unit of work produced as coursework.

The Controlled Test

Towards the end of the course, you will be expected to complete a controlled test (or externally set assignment) that is set by your examination board. This takes the form of a paper, which provides a choice of set 'starting points' for work.

You will be given the controlled test paper at least four weeks before the examination day(s) and must choose one of the options. There is a separate paper for each endorsement and one for the unendorsed study option.

In the time between being given the paper and the actual exam, you need to do as much preparatory work as possible. Conduct plenty of research and explore any different ideas you might have. This work can be carried out at home and at school and your teacher will be able to offer you guidance.

At the end of this period there will be a timed test lasting for ten hours in total. During this time you are expected to produce a final piece based upon your preparatory studies and research. For the duration of the test, you must work under exam conditions and can not be given any assistance.

You may work on your preparatory studies right up until the end of the timed test, at the end of which they must be handed in along with your final piece. Preparing for and taking the controlled test is looked at in more detail on pages 102-106.

▼ An example of a unit of work produced in a controlled test.

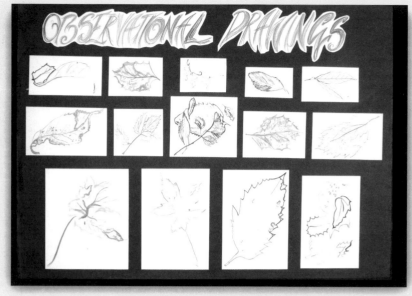

Assessment Objective 1

You need to record observations, experiences and ideas in forms that are appropriate to intentions.

To fulfil this objective you need to show that you can use both primary and secondary sources to gather relevant information. Relevance is the key word here. You must be able to make accurate judgements and decide whether a piece of information is appropriate or not. There is no point collecting lots of information if it is not going to help you develop your own work. Aim for quality not quantity.

You will also need to make records of your own ideas, observations and experiences. You need to record them in a way that both you (when you refer back to them) and others can clearly understand. There are lots of ways of doing this. Explore as many as possible, just make sure the ones that you use are suitable for the work you are producing.

Assessment

▲ Sketches (*shown above*) and photographs (*foot of page*) are an excellent way to record your observations.
▲ A few concise notes can make images easier to understand.

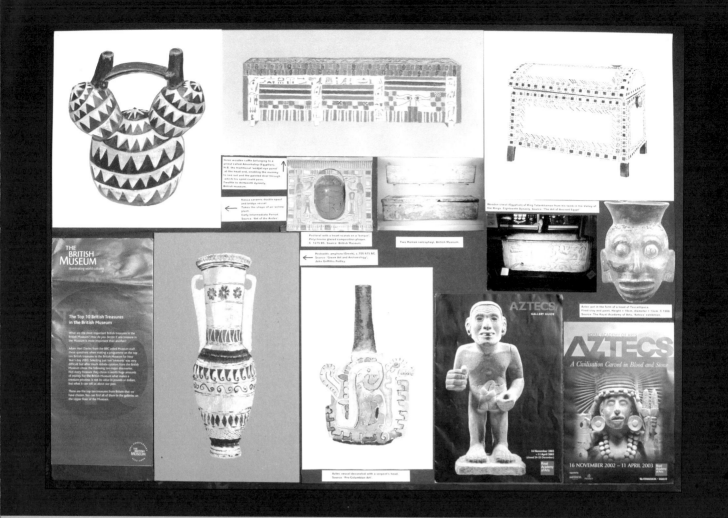

▲ Dedicated exhibitions, which comprise lots of different objects, can help to build an understanding of a particular culture or period in history.

▼ Look at images and objects relevant to your own work. This student, working in mixed media, examined the work of Rauschenberg, who developed a form of collage called 'combine painting'.

▼ A mounted sheet looking at the treatment of the reclining nude figure by different artists and movements.

Assessment Objective 2

You need to be able to analyse and evaluate images, objects and artefacts showing understanding of context.

To fulfil this objective you need to be able to look at work, by both past and contemporary artists, and assess it critically, with reference to the time and culture in which it was produced. To do this, you will need to research the background of the piece and gain a good understanding of why and how the artist produced it. You could look at what his/her motives and influences were, whether the piece is exemplary of a particular movement or style, how the piece might have been received at that time etc.

The examiner will also be looking to see whether you can understand and use the specialist vocabulary used in art and design. You will come across lots of specialist terms in your research. Make sure you know exactly what they mean before you attempt to use them yourself.

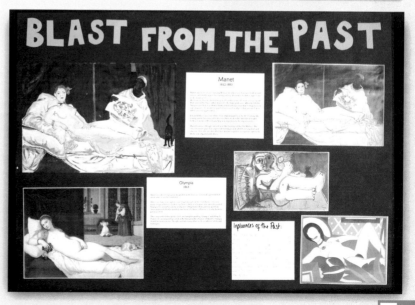

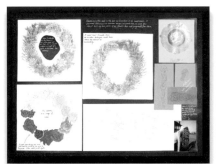

Assessment Objective 3

You need to develop and explore ideas using media, processes and resources, reviewing, modifying and refining work as it progresses.

This assessment objective allows you to demonstrate to the examiner how creative and versatile you are. You need to start with an idea or theme and develop it, exploring lots of possible solutions using different materials, techniques and processes. This will show off the range and depth of your skills and help you to discover which media and methods allow you to communicate your ideas most effectively.

During these investigations, you should constantly be evaluating your work. You will need to discard some examples and select others for further development. Those that you select need to be modified and refined until you are entirely satisfied with the results. This whole process should be apparent to the examiner.

◀ This student explores one idea, involving a wreath
▼ of flowers, before discarding it and moving on to another design idea. In the process, she experiments with stencilling, heat transfer, silk painting and embroidery.

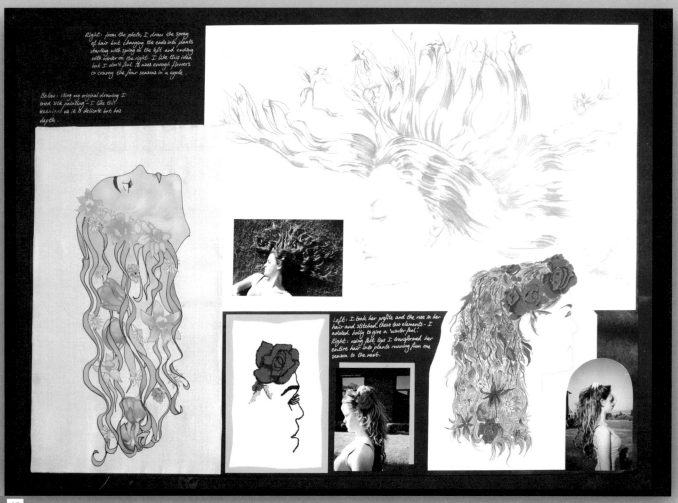

Assessment Objective 4

You need to be able to present a personal response, realising intentions and making informed connections with the work of others.

This final objective looks at all your work as a complete package; the examiner will view all your preparatory work together with the final piece as an entire unit. They will be looking to see if you have successfully achieved what you set out to do - you should have produced a final piece that completely satisfies all the criteria of your chosen starting point or theme. They will also be looking for originality - work that is unique and personal to you.

The examiner should be able to see connections between your own work and the work of other artists. Whatever you learned through your analysis of images, objects and artefacts (see Assessment Objective 2, page 9) should be put to good practical use and clearly reflected in your own work.

▲ This student studied cubism in her preparatory work and
▼ produced paintings and photographs of flamenco dancers

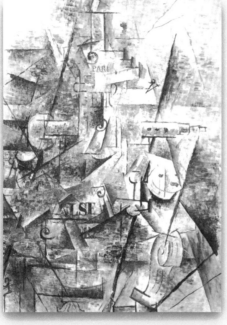

▶ The final piece, a cubist sculpture of a flamenco dancer clearly reflects her studies and research.

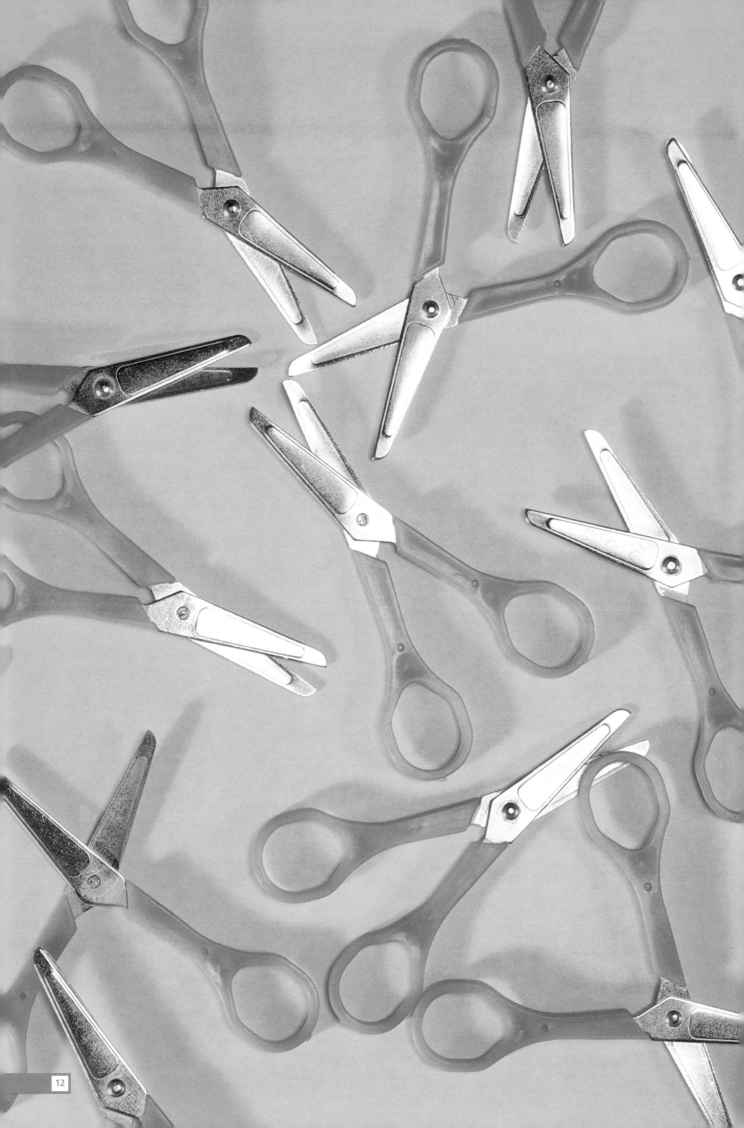

Knowledge and Skills

There are four key criteria against which all Art and Design students are assessed, irrespective of their examination board and the endorsement or study area(s) that they choose to work in. You must have an understanding of ...

- ... How ideas, feelings and meanings are conveyed in images and artefacts.
- ... A range of art, craft and design processes in two and/or three dimensions.
- ... How images and artefacts relate to their social, historical and cultural context.
- ... The approaches, methods and intentions of contemporary practitioners and those from different times and cultures, and their contribution to continuity and change in art, craft and design.

You must demonstrate knowledge, skills and a clear understanding of all four areas in *both* your coursework *and* controlled test.

You must provide clear evidence of your investigations in these areas. As well as thoroughly researching these subjects, it is essential that you practise any new skills and procedures and demonstrate what you have learned in your work.

Display your findings in a plain and simple way and develop your thoughts and ideas in a logical manner. Remember, you need to communicate what you have learned to a third party (the examiner). Leave nothing to chance - use notes and annotations to direct them to specific pieces on your sheets or in your

workbook and explain what they show. This is much better than leaving the examiner to try and piece together random examples of work by themselves and draw their own conclusions.

There are no set rules on how to approach these four areas and communicate your findings. In the next few pages they are looked at in more detail to help give you some ideas.

Ideas, Feelings and Meanings

▲ Abstract art is the opposite of figurative art. It relies on colour, shape and the visual elements to express a feeling or idea.

One of the main aims of this course is to help you improve your creative thought processes and expand your powers of imagination. Alongside this, you will need to develop your practical skills so that you can communicate your ideas and express your feelings successfully through art, craft and design.

For each unit of work you will have a starting point. This could be a specific design brief or something more open-ended like a theme to explore (see pages 86-87). Many artists produce work based around a topical, social, political, religious or ethical issue. This makes their work accessible to a wide audience whilst allowing them to express a personal viewpoint.

Don't panic if you aren't immediately struck by inspiration. Start by conducting a bit of research around the subject - this should help to generate different ideas for work. You only need a couple of good ideas to get you started. As you explore and develop these further, you will find that more and more possibilities occur to you. Once you get into the habit of creative thinking, new ideas will come into your head all the time. Make sure you take a notebook with you wherever you go so that you can jot them down as and when you think of them.

Discuss your ideas with other people. Teachers, family and friends, representing the different sexes and various age groups, will all have different ways of thinking and might have some interesting suggestions for developing your ideas further.

Art and design is essentially about expressing ideas through a visual medium. There is no point having great ideas if you cannot put them into practice and communicate them effectively to a third party. To help you do this, look at work produced by different historical and contemporary practitioners. Investigate how they approached a particular project, brief or theme and how they generated their ideas. Then look at the resultant work. How do they communicate their ideas? In your opinion, are their methods effective? Do not be afraid to criticise their work. If you do not like something, note down what you would change and why.

Look at the style of the piece - some artists choose to create an image that portrays their ideas in a direct and figurative way, whilst others prefer to use abstract colour and form to capture the essence of a mood or feeling.

Look for symbolism - animals, flowers, symbols etc. can represent different things in different cultures and faiths. For example, the dove is a universally recognised symbol of

peace and the lily is used to signify purity in some religious art.

Think carefully about the materials that have been used, the techniques that have been employed and the different visual elements e.g. colour, line and tone (see pages 22-32). These things will all have a significant impact on the way in which a piece of work is perceived.

Many pieces of artwork appear straightforward on first viewing but when you consider the origins and background they take on new meaning. Do a bit of research into allegory in art. This can help you to identify and understand characters and events used by some artists to represent a moral or spiritual idea.

Now you can apply what you have learned to your own work. It is up to you to use your findings to maximum effect and communicate your ideas and feelings to the audience.

▲ Figurative or representational art portrays things that we recognise as real from the world around us.

◀ Art with a religious theme often incorporates symbolism. This angel holding a stem of lilies represents purity and virtue .

▼ This student used the Statue of Liberty, a famous American emblem representing freedom, as the basis of this political piece. The supporting sketchbook pages show how he developed his ideas.

Within your chosen endorsement, you will be expected to produce the widest possible range of work. You might be limited by the materials and facilities available to you within the Art and Design department at your college / school and the specialisms of the teaching staff, however you should still find plenty of scope for exploration.

You ought to be able to use materials commonly available in school art departments, including coloured pencils, felt-tip pens, wax crayons, pencils, paint, graphite sticks, pastels, chalks, inks and charcoal. Where appropriate you should also try to experiment with a wider range of materials, for example clay, wood, metal, stone, photography, textiles, printmaking and ICT.

When using different materials, try to be as thorough as possible in your investigations. Often something as simple as using different qualities and colours of paper can have a strong visual impact.

Try to experiment with both two- and three-dimensional work and a variety of scales. This demonstrates that you can realise your ideas using space, volume, shape and form. With every piece of work you produce, try to be

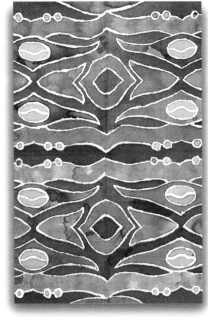
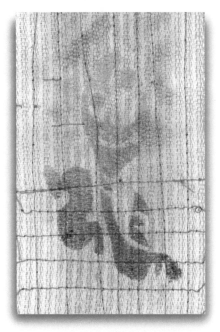
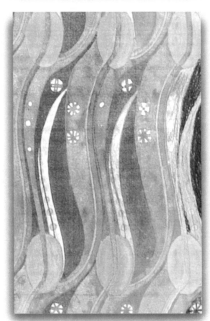
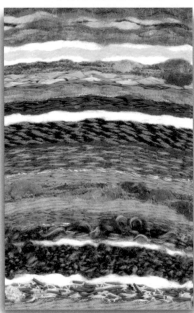

▼ Experiment with combining different materials

Different Art.

aware of all the visual elements (pages 22-32).

Make sure you include explanations and descriptions of all the different techniques and processes you have explored, to show that you have fully addressed this course criteria. You are unlikely to use them all in the final piece, so it is vital that you provide evidence of your research and preliminary work.

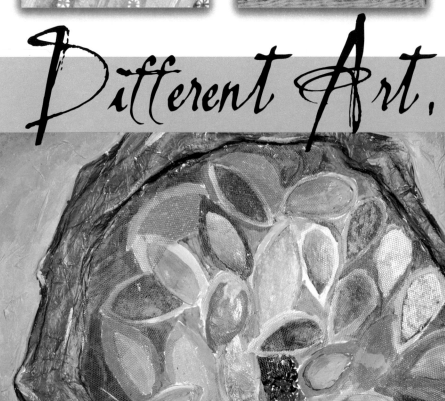

Craft and Design Processes

All the different materials, techniques and processes should be recorded in your sketchbook. Most students present the relevant ones on mounted sheets when they submit their work for assessment.

It is important to study historical practices as well as contemporary ones to fully understand how they have developed and the impact that this has had on the work that artists, designers and crafts people can produce. You may discover a process that you want to explore further in your own work or decide to experiment with a traditional technique that you had not previously considered. To get the highest marks possible, make sure you explain how this affects your way of working and the results that you achieve.

Generally speaking, the more materials, techniques and processes you demonstrate, the better your marks will be. However, to achieve the highest marks you need to demonstrate these elements skilfully. It is not enough just to dabble with a technique, you need to study it in depth and practise until you can apply it confidently.

▲ Used appropriately, ICT applications can be classed as art and design processes.
▲ Producing small test pieces is an excellent way to try out different techniques and develop new skills (*see textiles pieces on facing page also*).

Other Practitioners' Work

Throughout this course you should grow and develop as an artist or designer. One of the best ways to improve your methods of working and help you to develop a personal style is to study other practitioners (i.e. artists, craftspeople and designers).

Contemporary practitioners can be found working in a variety of fields, producing incredibly diverse work. They draw upon a range of influences from different times and places. Some use traditional techniques whilst others take advantage of the newest materials and technology. The variety is so great, it would be virtually impossible not to find someone who produces work that appeals to you. It is your responsibility to conduct some research and find that artist or designer whose work and methods will influence and inspire you.

You do not necessarily have to study the acknowledged masters (i.e. famous artists whose work is displayed in national collections around the world). There are lots of lesser-known practitioners who produce good quality work. To earn good marks in this area, be prepared to go and search out these people. There are a host of art festivals, craft shows, local galleries and exhibitions, trade fairs etc. where you will find people displaying their work and demonstrating their skills. There are also more formal events e.g. where an artist or designer is invited to give a talk.

▲ These students have studied the work of Friedrich, Van Gogh and Lichtenstein (top row, left to right), and then gone on to produce original pieces in the same style.

◄ Museums and galleries are good places to study the work of other practitioners firsthand.

Don't be afraid to pick up the telephone and contact a particular artist. Be polite, explain what you are doing and that you are interested in their work. If they seem forthcoming, ask if it would be possible to meet them in person or visit their studio. By studying these people firsthand, you will get a much better idea of the creative process and their working methods.

You should consider trying to arrange some work-based training or volunteering as an unpaid assistant at a local art or design studio. Other industrial or commercial establishments might also be worth approaching depending upon your specific interests. Past students have produced work influenced by visits to interior design studios, foundries, ceramic tile factories, theatre costume departments, landscape design offices, television production units, glass-blowing workshops etc. all to good effect.

Alternatively, you may prefer the more traditional approach of studying the work produced by past and contemporary practitioners in museums and galleries. Some institutions like this have specialist research facilities and archive material, which students can use for further study on request.

Studying the work of other practitioners can help you to understand the complex role played by the artist in society. Hopefully you will begin to appreciate how the work of individuals contributes to the bigger picture and the impact it can have on the world of art.

▼ This mounted sheet includes photographs, sketches and notes made during a visit to a sculpture park.

▲ These photos document a visit to Diana Hall's ceramics workshop.

Researching the social, historical and cultural context of a piece can help you to develop a better understanding of why and how it was produced. It can also illuminate factors that influence your own work, which you might not have considered before.

From the dawn of man, peoples from all around the world have been producing images and artefacts. Historically, these are invaluable, not just for their aesthetic merits but because of what they tell us about the lifestyle and beliefs of the people who created them and the events that were taking place at that time.

People from different continents often produce very different work, so it is important that you look at examples from all around the world (not just the UK and Western Europe), preferably at firsthand in a museum or gallery. You may find that the materials, techniques and processes they use can be incorporated into your own work effectively. For the benefit of the examiner, highlight how you have done this.

When studying work from different periods and cultures, not only should

Inner wooden coffin belonging to a priest called Amenhotep (Egyptian). N.B. the traditional 'wedjat-eye panel' at the head end, enabling the mummy to see out and the painted door through which his spirit could pass.
Twelfth to thirteenth dynasty, British museum.

▲ This student needs to know something about the beliefs of Ancient Egyptians to understand the significance of the symbols on this coffin.

Social, Historical

you look at how it was produced, you also need to investigate why it was produced. The religious, ritual and social aspects of a culture or time are often reflected in the work it produces. In books and museums, you will find visual records of important events, ceremonial artefacts, emblems of community spirit and pieces depicting rites of passage. Don't neglect pieces like this as a source of artistic inspiration.

To fully cover this assessment criteria, it is not enough to simply download life histories of artists or reproduce

▶ This mixed media piece makes a direct comment about current global events and issues. Past practitioners have used art for similar purposes.

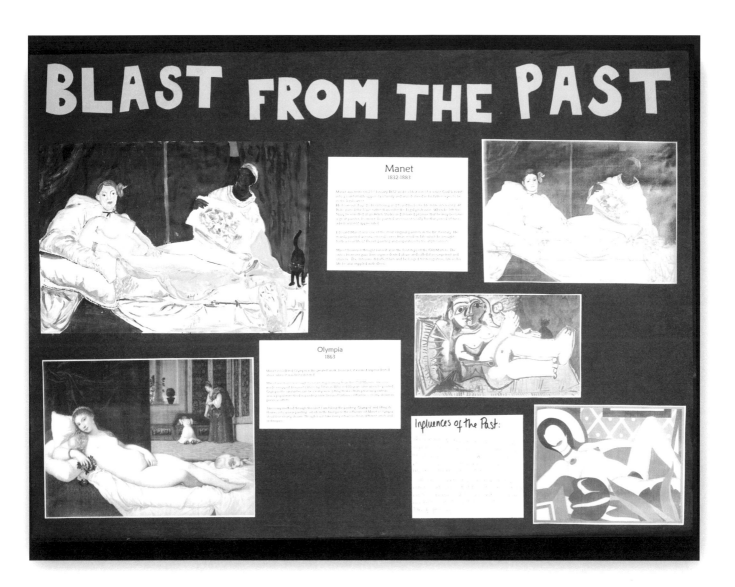

BLAST FROM THE PAST

Manet
1832-1883

Olympia
1863

Influences of the Past:

and Cultural Context ▲

This student has looked at the reclining nude in the context of different historic periods and how it was received by society at those times.

designs from a particular culture or movement. You will need to learn about different cultures and historical events to fully understand the motivation and meaning behind different pieces. To do this you will need to look beyond the classroom. It may involve a little extra effort on your behalf, but you should find it very rewarding.

Do not restrict yourself to historical pieces either. Contemporary pieces can be just as interesting when studied in a social and cultural context. Try looking at work by local and national artists or designers to see what their work says about the area where you live and this country.

▶ With a bit of research, stylised patterns and motifs, like this Viking one, often reveal something about the culture that produced them.

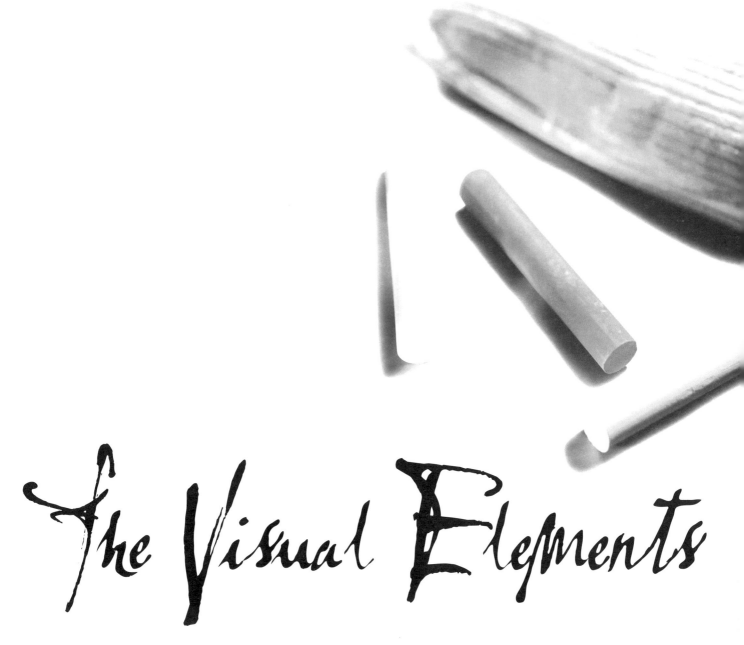

The Visual Elements

All Art and Design students need a good working knowledge of the 'Visual Elements'. These are the basic physical components that make-up a piece of art and design:

• Colour
• Line
• Tone
• Texture
• Shape and Form

You need to understand how each element can be used and manipulated to produce different effects in your work and affect the way in which it is perceived by a third party. The best way to learn about these things is to look at how other artists employ them.

Once you understand the theory, you can then work towards developing your practical skills. You should be able to use these elements in your own work to maximum effect; to communicate your ideas effectively.

The following pages look at each of the elements in turn and should help you to understand just some of the ways they can be utilised in your work.

Colour

▼ Different colours can dramatically change the overall effect of an image.

▲ Colour can be used in an abstract way to create mood, movement and texture.

Throughout this course, you must demonstrate a sound knowledge of colour and colour theory. You need to know the names of colours, the different types of colour and how to mix colours.

You will have some knowledge of colour when you start this course, but your understanding needs to be much more specialised at GCSE level.

There are three key colours in an artist's palette: red, yellow and blue. These are called the **Primary Colours** because they cannot be mixed from other colours. In theory, these are the only colours you need, as all other colours can be mixed from them.

Secondary Colours are produced when two primary colours are mixed in equal quantities:

> **Red + Blue = Violet**
> **Blue +** Yellow **= Green**
> Yellow **+ Red =** Orange

Tertiary Colours are produced when a primary colour and a secondary colour are mixed.

A **Colour Wheel** (see facing page) is a very useful tool. It can help you to understand these ideas and apply them to your own work.

Three basic terms are used to describe colour: hue, saturation and tone. These can be dealt with individually, but they all work in conjunction with each other.

Hues are defined by the 'redness', 'yellowness' or 'blueness' of a colour. For example, scarlet and crimson are both hues of red. Crimson is more 'blue' and Scarlet is more 'yellow' (see diagram on facing page). Scientific research suggests that the human eye can perceive around 150 differences in hue.

Saturation describes the purity or intensity of a colour.

Tone can be changed by making a colour lighter or darker. When white is added to a colour it produces a tint (or lighter hue) and decreases the colour saturation. When black is added it produces a shade (or darker hue) and decreases the colour saturation.

Colours also have different qualities and properties. You need to recognise these and be able to use them to effect in your work

Complementary (or Contrasting) Colours are those directly opposite each other on the colour wheel. Placed next to each other, the intensity of two complementary colours will appear to increase.

Analogous (or Harmonious) Colours are side by side on the colour wheel.

Warm Colours appear on the right-hand side of the colour wheel e.g. red, orange and yellow.

Cool Colours appear on the left-hand side of the colour wheel e.g. blue, green and indigo.

Advancing Colours appear to come towards you. These tend to be warm or saturated colours.

Receding Colours sink away from you. These tend to be cool or less saturated colours.

Colour carries powerful symbolism. It can be used to project a mood, evoke emotion or create drama. For example, red is a hot colour often used to show passion, blues and yellows can be dynamic and exciting, and browns, greens and other 'natural' colours can have a calming effect.

Artists, designers and craftspeople all use these concepts in their work. Graphic designers use them to sell products, theatre designers use them to create illusions on stage, textile and fashion designers use them to create eye-catching and flattering designs and landscape painters use them to create atmospheric perspective and a sense of distance.

Experimenting with colour theory can lead you to some surprising discoveries, which will have a dramatic effect on the work you produce. Also, if you understand these theories, you can look at existing work in a gallery or museum and really begin to appreciate the complexities of the art, without even understanding the subject or the title of a piece.

The Colour Wheel

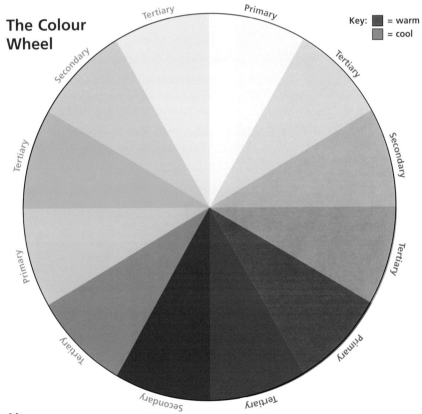

Key: ■ = warm ■ = cool

The colour wheel on this page applies to artists pigments such as oil, gauche, watercolour, dye, acrylics etc. If you have chosen one of the more specialist study areas, you will need to understand the difference between the colours used when working with art pigments, printing inks / dyes and light.

Four-Colour Process Printing (CMYK), uses three primary colours, cyan, magenta and yellow, in conjunction with black.

Coloured Light (e.g. stage lighting and computer or television screens) has three primary colours, red, blue and green, which produce white light when added together.

Hue

◀ This diagram shows different hues of red. Scarlet is on the yellow side of red and crimson is on the blue side.

Tone

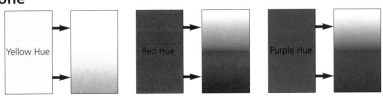

Yellow Hue

Red Hue

Purple Hue

◀ You can achieve different tones by adding white to lighten a hue and black to darken it. Light tones are called *tints*, dark tones are called *shades*.

For centuries, artists, designers and crafts people have relied upon their ability to express thoughts, ideas and feelings with a simple line.

Lines are not just marks made using a pencil or pen - the range of media available to you is huge, providing endless ways in which to express yourself. Likewise, when making a linear mark, there are limitless variations possible. The weight and thickness of the line and the way in which you apply a particular medium can express a great deal. Swelling and tapering lines can provide contours, depth and a feeling of space, whilst the way in which marks are placed, the vigour with which they are applied and their fluency or tentativeness can all communicate different things and vastly alter the overall effect.

The way in which different marks are arranged and link together can be very revealing. Fluency can sometimes reflect whether an artist is creating an image from a subject in front of them or from their imagination. The ways in which lines flow, break, join and overlap can also create illusions of depth or solidity of

▲ These goldfish are drawn in a style influenced by oriental art, using fluid lines well suited to the subject matter.

▼ Lines of stitching are used to create movement in this piece.

Line

form. Combinations of methods can also be successful e.g. combining linear lines for outlining with broad strokes, cross-hatching and sweeping gestures for filling and shading.

Pencils, paints, inks, pastels, chalks, crayons, felt-tip pens, graphite sticks, charcoal etc. can all be used to make a range of marks. Broaden your horizons in this area. Etching, carving, incising, scratching, stitching, chiseling etc. all create line and when combined with different materials can create endless possibilities.

▲ The designs for etchings are produced using a sharp needle, creating characteristic fine lines and cross-hatching.

In addition, the examiner will expect you to demonstrate a range of styles. A simple tool like a pencil can be used in a multitude of ways. Experiment with using different grades and by applying different pressures; try using a dabbing motion or cross-hatching marks to produce different surface qualities; contrast a flowing line with more angular marks…

Make sure you look at the way in which different practitioners have used line in the past, it should give you ideas for further experimentation.

Artists like Picasso, Dürer, Degas and Matisse are famous for their lively, experimental work in this field and their passion for trying to capture exact feelings and moods has inspired many others. You can also look at images in advertising, on packaging, on printed and constructed textiles, across sheet metal construction, in printmaking etc. They all rely on fluidity and application of line to communicate different ideas.

▶ This caricature uses thick felt-tip lines for outlining, and finer lines for shading.

Tone refers to the gradation from light to dark on the surface of an object when light falls upon it. It is often used to refer to colour (see pages 24-25), but it also applies to pieces where no colour is used at all. It is particularly important in giving depth to two-dimensional images like photographs and drawings.

Tonal work will help you to understand forms and sketch images quickly. Again, there is a wide variety of materials and approaches available to you. Charcoal, pencil, pastels, brush and ink wash etc. can all be used to capture the essence of a form quickly and effectively.

Tone can create tremendous mood and atmosphere in a piece. It can be used to express flat planes of light and areas of shadow without using linear marks at all. To help understand tone, try half closing your eyes and looking at an object through your eye lashes. This slightly blurs the lines of the image and allows the areas of light and dark to stand out.

Initially, it helps to flood the object you are studying with light from a single source. This will make it easier for you to see, providing clear areas of strong light and dark shadow. The difficulty comes when studying the transitional tones from light to dark and portraying them accurately. A certain amount of subtlety is required. It often helps to build up these areas gradually, adding layer upon layer until the desired effect is achieved. You might also experiment with using an eraser to lighten areas of a pencil drawing.

You will have no difficulties finding existing examples of art and design that demonstrate good use of tone. Artists such as Rembrandt and Caravaggio used extreme light and dark in some of their compositions to illuminate a particular section of the painting and enhance its dramatic effect. The technical term for balancing light and shadow in this way is 'Chiaroscuro' or 'Clair-Obscur'.

Tone

▲ Because there is an absence of colour, black and white photography allows you to focus on tone.
▼ This silk-painting uses different hues and tones of the same colour to show areas of light and dark.

▼ These drawings all show a good understanding of tone, helping to give them a three-dimensional quality.

▲ Impressionists, like Monet, are famous for their work, which attempts to perfectly capture tone and the quality of light at one particular moment.

Texture

▼ A fibrous paper and excellent tonal skills create the illusion of texture in this drawing of a celtic cross.

▲ This textiles piece uses beads, netting and different fabrics to create lots of contrasting textures.

Texture refers to the surface quality of an object. It can also be used to describe the material qualities of a piece, such as the planished surface on a metal object, the rhythm of the brush strokes in a loosely handled painting, the knitted surface of a piece of textiles, the chisel marks on a piece of carved sculpture. Likewise, it can refer to the illusion of texture in a piece e.g. the impression of fine hair on a rabbit, the roughness of bark on a tree or the smooth skin of an apple in a painting. You need to explore all these ideas in your coursework.

You can recreate and enhance the surface quality of your subject depending on the materials you use and the way you treat them:

A fine artist might add various materials to a base medium to create different surface qualities. Sand, sawdust, decorator's caulk etc. can all

be added to paint to give texture to the work when the paint dries.

Textiles artists and designers can take advantage of the wide range of different fabrics and materials e.g. silk, satin, wool, velvet and corduroy.

Sculptors use a variety of tools to shape and form their work. The way in which they work with those tools will determine the surface texture and mood of the final piece. Chisels, scrapers, rifflers and mechanical polishers can all leave a different finish.

Three-dimensional designers who work in metal can coat their finished piece to protect it and to create a different appearance. They could galvanize, paint, powder coat or varnish their work.

Look at existing pieces of art to see how effectively the illusion of texture can be achieved in two-dimensional pieces. The fur of the hare in Dürer's famous drawing is meticulously handled with the artist seemingly drawing each hair. In contrast, Rembrandt's fast, generous strokes of paint allowed him to portray lace and fabric quickly and spontaneously.

Experiment with different combinations of materials and techniques to explore the different textures that can be achieved. You need to spend some time working with each combination to really investigate their qualities and earn good marks.

▶ These small ceramic test pieces explore how pattern and glaze can be used to produce different textures.

▼ Papier Mâché, netting and sequins give texture to this mixed-media piece.

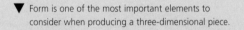
These two ceramic pieces have the same function but take very different forms.

Shape and form are both words that can be used to describe the external appearance of an object, as distinct from its colour, texture, tone etc. Shape tends to be used to refer to the two-dimensional aspect of an object, as defined by its outline, and form is applied to the three-dimensional aspect or configuration.

Together, shape and form are often used to talk about the way in which the different visual elements are combined within a piece of art or design. On this course, you are expected to study and explore lots of different areas of art and design. You then need to be able to bring all of these things together in a thoughtful way to create work that is visually pleasing.

The art of combining the various elements of a drawing, painting, photograph, sculpture etc. is called composition. In a good composition the various shapes and forms are arranged so that the work continues to hold the viewer's interest well after its initial impact. When you look at a well composed image you should feel that everything is balanced and harmonious.

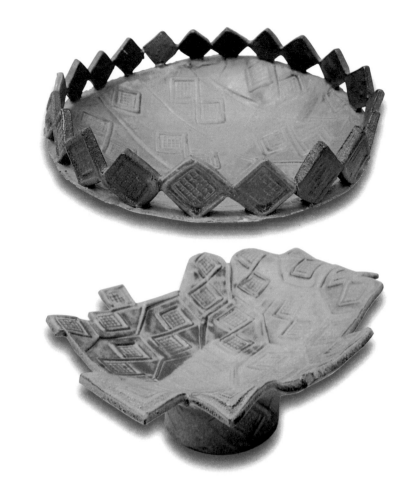

▼ Form is one of the most important elements to consider when producing a three-dimensional piece.

▼ Experiment with different compositions until you are completely satisfied.

▲ These prints are two-dimensional but clever use of scale makes the larger objects in the foreground appear closer. Yellow is an advancing colour, which accentuates this effect in the print on the right.

Shape and Form

Look at work by various artists and designers, past and present, to see how they achieve a satisfying effect. The ancient Greeks were so obsessed with this idea that they actually developed a formula, called the 'Golden Section' or Golden Mean', which could be used in pieces of art and design to create perfect visual harmony and proportion. With a bit of research you can find lots of examples where it has been applied, particularly in neo-classical art and architecture. You will also find that some practitioners purposefully disregard these ideas of balance and harmony to achieve dramatic effects.

In your own work you should try experimenting with different viewpoints and exploring different shapes of paper, canvas etc. Breaking away from the traditional landscape or portrait format can produce some interesting results.

To earn the best marks possible, you need to explore all the different elements and techniques that can affect and aid composition. Make sure you investigate perspective, size and scale and the ideas of positive and negative space. Try out different ways of creating space and volume and practise making two-dimensional images appear three-dimensional.

▲ The arrangement of the two haystacks in this painting by Monet create depth and balance. Although more subtle, the position of the horizon is also important.

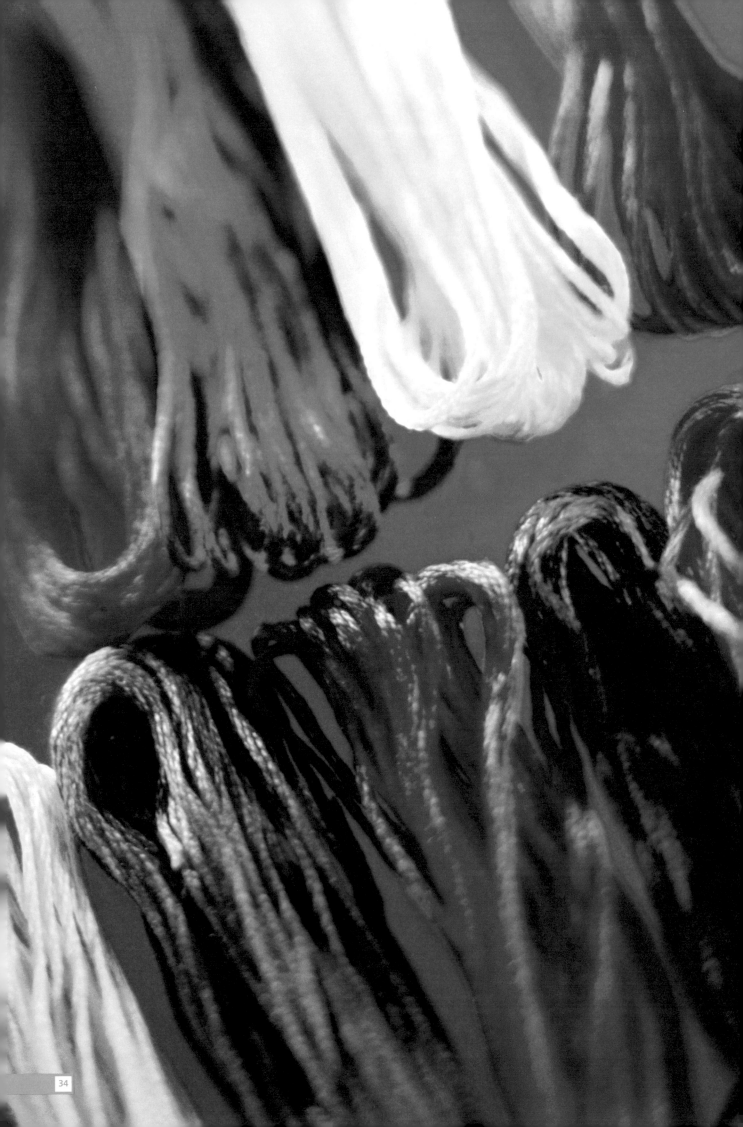

The Endorsements

If you are following the full GCSE Art and Design course, you have to choose from one of six course options (as detailed on page 5). There are five 'endorsed' courses. This simply means that you choose to specialise and work within one discipline for the entire course: fine art, textile design, graphic design, three-dimensional design or photography. The sixth option is the unendorsed course, which allows you to produce work in two or more of the listed disciplines.

Regardless of the option you choose, if you successfully complete the course you will be awarded a qualification in GCSE Art and Design.

You may find that your school limits the options available to you. This is normally because they only have the facilities, resources and teaching staff available to cover certain options at the required level.

There isn't any one course that is better than the others. It all comes down to personal preference and what you want to get out of the course.

An endorsed course will allow you to explore one discipline in greater depth. You will gain a good knowledge of its history and the artists who practice it and you can really come to grips with the different materials and processes, developing your skills and expertise.

The unendorsed course, on the other hand, will allow you to explore and compare different disciplines. You can work towards mastering a range of skills and increasing your versatility as an artist.

Following an endorsed course may seem restrictive in comparison to the unendorsed option. However, each discipline encompasses a number of different study areas and covers a huge range of materials and processes.

The following section looks at each course option in turn and examines it in detail. It explores the skills and elements which are unique to that course and looks at the different areas of work that it covers. This should help you to understand the requirements of each course and the creative possibilities it offers.

Please note, all students taking the short GCSE Art and Design course must follow the unendorsed course.

Fine Art

Introduction to Fine Art

Fine Art is the communication of your ideas, feelings and observations through a visual medium. Your final piece should purely be a reflection of your personal experiences. This is unlike Applied or Decorative Art, which often has a practical purpose, beginning with a brief and ending with the production of an object that has a specific function.

The main focus of Fine Art is your thoughts and emotions. However, you are also expected to conduct relevant research and demonstrate a wide variety of practical skills.

Hopefully, in your research, you will discover work by other artists that interests and inspires you. It might help you to look at the world around you in a different way and encourage you to experiment with new techniques in your own work.

As you work, keep the examiner in mind. It is important to show them how you have developed your ideas. They will also be looking to see how much you know about your chosen study area and what practical skills you have.

If you are studying Fine Art, you need to read the information in this section carefully AND the 'Essential Skills and Learning' section at the front of this book (pages 12-32) to make sure you cover all the requirements for the GCSE Art and Design course.

You must produce work within one or more of the following study areas: Drawing and/or Painting, Sculpture, Land Art or Installation, Printmaking, Film or Video, Mixed Media. You will find more information about the individual subject areas on pages 41-45.

Recording Images

▲ Photography can be a quick and convenient way to record what you see.

▼ Observational drawings allow you to record specific details that interest you.

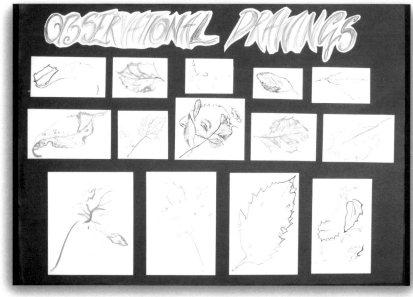

Although you must include some written notes and annotation, you should remember that the examiner only has limited time to assess your coursework, so avoid lengthy pieces of text. The most effective way to record and communicate your observations, ideas and feelings is through images.

Images can be observational, analytical, expressive or imaginative.

Observational work is an excellent starting point for any project and should be an integral part of your work. Taking a photograph can be a convenient way of recording what you see, but large quantities of photographs will not earn you many marks on their own.

Photographs show what you see, but not *how* you see it. Observational drawings are more personal and therefore of far greater value. You can use them to show the audience the things that interest and attract you e.g. shape, texture or tone.

Analytical work can help you develop an understanding of another artist's work. By reproducing one of their pieces (make sure you credit them clearly, see page 92) or emulating their style, you can explore the techniques they employ and gain a better insight into their work.

Rather than produce an image that is a direct representation of something that you have seen, it is possible to create an image entirely (or partly) from your imagination. It could feature 'real' or fantasy elements or a combination of both - there really are no boundaries. Imagination and creativity are an important part of this endorsement.

Your images do not need to be representational or figurative i.e. they do not need to portray something recognisable. It is just as valid, and often more effective, to produce an abstract image to express a feeling, emotion or mood.

You should aim to include examples of all these different approaches in your coursework. This will demonstrate your versatility as an artist and show the examiner that you have explored different avenues in the development of your final piece.

Different Ways of Working

You need to explore different ways of working and demonstrate that you can use a wide range of materials, techniques, equipment and processes relevant to your chosen area of study. Experiment with materials and mediums that you haven't used before. Don't be afraid to ask your teacher or another artist to demonstrate an unfamiliar product or technique to you.

Pencils

Pencils are readily available and easy to use. Hard (H grade) and soft (B grade) pencils can produce very different results. A scale is used to show the relative hardness and softness of pencils. HB (a standard pencil) is the fixed point on the scale, from which other pencils are numbered e.g. 3H, 2H, H, HB, B, 2B, 3B etc. the higher the number the harder or softer the pencil is. Hard leads produce clean, fine lines and are good for technical drawing. Soft leads produce heavier lines that can be smudged like charcoal.

Paper

Different types and grades of paper can produce diverse effects. For example, watercolour paper has a thick, fibrous surface, which is ideal for absorbing paint. Pastels work well with texture, which enhances their quality; wrapping paper or lightly grained paper (e.g. Ingres) are excellent choices. Paper doesn't have to be costly, try experimenting with sugar paper, newspaper or making your own.

Paints

There is a wide range of paints available, each with its own distinctive quality. Traditionally, oil paint and acrylic are popular with artists. Watercolours, applied in thin washes of colour, are more delicate. Don't forget to try out less common alternatives e.g. gouache (which is popular with designers) and tempera (which was used by many of the Masters).

Modelling Materials

A wide variety of structural materials can be used for three-dimensional pieces. Card, plaster of Paris, papier mâché, wire, wood and metal are all readily available. Be as innovative as you like in your hunt for materials. Everyday objects e.g. empty drinks cans, bubble-wrap and textiles can produce interesting results. Other materials like clay, stone and plastic might be less easy to get hold of and require specialist equipment.

Other Materials

There is a vast array of artists' materials to explore. Other popular choices include pastels, wax crayons, chalk, charcoal, marker pens, coloured pencils and pen and ink.

ICT

You must demonstrate that you can use Information and Communications Technology (ICT) effectively. It may not be appropriate to digitally create and manipulate images in your chosen area of study, however, you can still use ICT to search for information and present your findings.

Language and Conventions

▲ Producing an original piece in the style of a famous artist or movement demonstrates an understanding of conventions. This portrait of an African woman mirrors the style of the Van Gogh self-portrait.

Language

Art has its own language and in your research you will probably come across lots of specialist terms. These might describe a style of art, a period in art history, a technique or even an idea.

You are not expected to know all these terms but you should be familiar with the ones that are relevant to your own work. You need to understand what they mean and be able to use them correctly.

When you come across an unfamiliar term, try to find out what it means. Many reference books have a glossary (a kind of dictionary) that can help you. Alternatively, you could look it up in a dictionary, on the Internet or ask your teacher.

If you are not clear about the meaning of an art term, don't use it.

Conventions

In your research you will come across art styles and movements that interest and inspire you e.g. Renaissance, Impressionism, Pop Art.

A reference book or Internet search can provide you with basic information about these styles and movements e.g. dates, country of origin, key style points. However, these should only be used as a starting point. To really understand the subject you will have to conduct your own investigations.

Begin by looking at works of art that are generally thought to be good examples of that style or movement. You should study them closely. Try to identify what they have in common. It might be…

• The materials and the way in which they are used
• The colours used
• The subject matter of the piece
• Common themes
• Reoccurring symbolism/motifs etc.

These are the things that will help you the most when it comes to producing your own work.

Composition

▲ Experiment with different compositions before finalising a design.

▲ This oversized bic lighter shows how playing with scale can be fun.

When an artist produces a piece of work, they combine all the different elements in a way that they find appropriate. This is called the composition. It is a very personal process and can therefore be difficult to understand.

The best way to explore composition is by looking at the work of other artists.

Pictorial Space

An artist has created pictorial space successfully if there appears to be 'depth' to an image, even though it was created on a flat surface. It is worth studying one, two or three point perspective to help you with this. These are all methods used to create a three-dimensional appearance.

A good way to explore pictorial space is to take a composition e.g. a still life arrangement of fruit, and try drawing it from various angles and viewpoints. Notice how this can produce dramatically different effects.

Look closely at techniques used by other artists to create pictorial space e.g. use of perspective, viewpoint, shadow and light.

Rhythm

Although rhythm is a quality usually associated with music, a sense of rhythm can be created in a piece of art through the arrangement of its elements. Depending on how an artist places solid masses alongside spaces, alternates

light and shadow or uses different colours in their work, they can produce a harmonious and flowing rhythm or one that is broken and abrupt.

Scale

Scale refers to the relative size and proportion of one thing to another.

The size and shape of your work can influence how other people perceive it. Experiment with creating work on a very small scale e.g. a maquette or postage stamp sized piece. Then try something on a much larger scale e.g. a large image of a small object. You could even try using different scales within the same piece e.g. a large mouse alongside a tiny elephant.

In this study area, a good knowledge and understanding of the technical aspects of art is essential.

The examiner will be looking closely at...

... Your choice of materials

... Technique

... Composition (including use of pictorial space, perspective, scale and rhythm)

... Use of colour, line, tone, texture and shape

This does not mean that you should be any less imaginative in your work. There is a wide variety of different surfaces available to you. In addition to all the different types of paper (see page 38), you should also consider canvas and less conventional surfaces for your paintings and drawings e.g. fabric, wood and stone.

Hunt around your art department and experiment with as many different materials as possible. Painting and drawing do not restrict you to working with just paint and pencils. Other possibilities include charcoal,

▲ A drawing of a dancer showing good use of tone.

Painting and Drawing

chalk, pastels and graphite sticks.

Different materials will produce different results. They will affect the marks you make on the paper/canvas and therefore, the way in which you express yourself. You need to decide which materials and techniques communicate your thoughts and ideas most effectively.

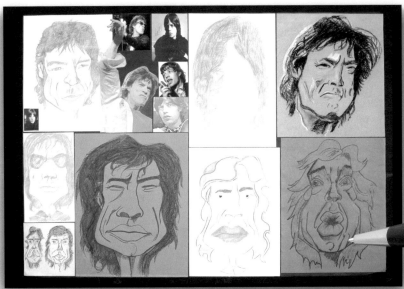

▲ Caricature studies of Mick Jagger produced using a range of materials.

If you choose this area of study, you should aim to develop a good basic knowledge of block, plate and screen-printing techniques. However, because printmaking often involves the use of specialist equipment, your options might be restricted by the facilities available at your school or college.

You need to learn about the technical side of printmaking and discover practical ways of translating your ideas into print.

Investigate the various finishes that can be achieved from different methods of printing and look at the processes that can be used to transfer images onto different surfaces such as paper, ceramic, fabric etc.

Eventually, you will need to select one of the following printing techniques to study in depth with a view to using it for the production of your final piece:

- Screen printing
- Mono printing
- Linocut
- Etching
- Lithography
- Dry point

Printmaking

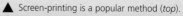

▲ Screen-printing is a popular method (*top*).
▲ This board shows mono printing being used in the development of ideas (*bottom left of board*).

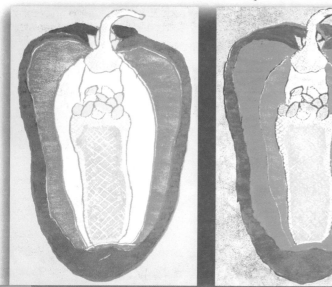

The examiner will be looking to see if you have chosen a technique appropriate to your work. To help you make this decision, you need to study the work of other printmakers. Find out about the techniques they used and evaluate the results - do you think their methods were effective? Try to be clear about your reasons for eliminating some methods and favouring others.

◄ Effective results can be achieved by combining printing techniques.

Sculpture, Installation etc.

In Sculpture, Land Art and/or Installation, you will need to produce three-dimensional forms, either full-size or in maquette form (i.e. as a model).

As a starting point for your work, you should research the formal elements of sculpture: volume, space, materials and movement. Look closely at the work of other artists to see how they address these elements in the pieces they produce. It will help you make decisions about your own work.

In addition to exploring a wide range of materials (pages 16-17), you will need to identify, practise and develop skills in suitable methods of construction. These could include soldering, brazing, welding, gluing, jointing, riveting, bolting or the manipulation of more plastic materials like perspex, clay, wax and synthetic modelling compounds.

You might also want to look at more complicated techniques such as casting or mould making.

Pay attention to detail! The surface quality of sculptural work is just as important as the form - a well chosen but unusual finish can produce striking results. Experiment with techniques like polishing, scouring, carving or cutting. In this study area particularly, it is a good idea to keep a photographic journal. Use a camera to document your progress stage by stage. This record could prove invaluable, especially if you are working with delicate or fragile materials or your work is of a transitory nature (i.e. temporary or impermanent like an ice sculpture for example).

▲ Photographic images and cubist studies are translated into an interesting three-dimensional, sculptural piece.

Although Film and Video comes under Fine Art, it may also be studied as part of Photography or Graphic Design depending upon your examination board and the nature of your work.

Digital technology is being used more and more in filmmaking so try to develop a clear understanding of what can be achieved using digital processes and how they work. You must be able to weigh up the advantages and disadvantages of digital technology against more traditional techniques when it comes to choosing production methods for your final piece.

You will need to produce storyboards and scripts for your films or videos. Before you begin, it is worth doing some research into this area. Look at formats and conventions used within the film industry.

Obviously, it is essential that you know how to use a camera competently. This includes a working knowledge of viewpoints, camera angles, compositions etc. You also need to understand the different requirements of interior and exterior filming, especially with regard to lighting and sound.

Good editing skills are equally important. You must learn how to cut a film using procedures like cropping, taking into account aspects such as pacing. The way in which a filmmaker mixes sound and vision is a complicated technique, which you will need to master.

Film and Video

▼ A storyboard is used to plan scenes and shots (*image courtesy of First Light*).

Mixed Media

Mixed media is the term used when an artist combines different materials within a single piece of work. This style became popular in the twentieth century when artists began challenging the established conventions of art and breaking down the barriers between the traditional disciplines.

To work with mixed media successfully, you will need to explore at least two other study areas of Fine Art:

- Painting / Drawing
- Sculpture, land art or installation
- Printmaking
- Film & Video

It is important that you are familiar with the skills and techniques within these areas, if you are to combine them effectively.

The list above is by no means final. You can investigate other fields of art and design that you feel are relevant to your work.

Because it is experimental, mixed media provides you with unlimited creative scope. Take advantage of this and be as imaginative as possible in your work.

If you don't know where to begin, try using painting or drawing as a starting point. Experiment by bringing in aspects of photography, printmaking, collage, low relief construction etc. As you see the exciting effects different combinations of materials can produce, new ideas and possibilities will open up to you.

Graphic Design

Introduction to Graphic Design

Graphic Design is about communicating a message through a visual medium, using text and images. The products of graphic design are often functional and include areas like advertising, product design and illustration.

Work within this endorsement frequently starts with a design brief, which will set out a particular problem for you to solve. Although design briefs impose constraints on your work, there is still plenty of scope to explore different design solutions and produce an original response.

In the design industry, briefs often specify a target audience, a budget, deadlines etc. and the resulting images or products are almost always intended for multiple reproduction.

You need to explore these and other factors that impact on the work of a designer (e.g. safety guidelines and legal issues) and apply similar considerations to your own work.

Because of the commercial aspect of Graphic Design, it can be very advantageous to gain some work experience or training within a design studio. This can provide you with an invaluable insight into the industry, which will benefit your work.

Within your portfolio the examiner will be looking for a good understanding of the design process, a methodical approach and creative awareness, as well as an ability to catch your audience's eye. You need to recognise current media trends

and technological advancements and be able to select and adapt them to fit your own purpose.

If you are studying Graphic Design, you need to read the information in this section AND the 'Essential Skills and Learning' section at the front of this book (pages 12-32) to make sure you cover all the requirements of the GCSE Art and Design course.

Depending on your examination board, you will be required to produce work in one or more of the following study areas (check what your options are with your teacher): Advertising and/or Packaging, Illustration, Typography, Printmaking, Computer-Aided Design and Digital Imaging, Film, Video and / or Animation.

Meaning, Function etc.

As a Graphic Designer, before you begin work it is essential that you fully understand the objective. You need to have an overview of the whole project - be clear about the message you want to convey, the function or purpose of the finished product and who your intended audience is. If you lose sight of this, the whole project will fail.

Your teacher will give you a brief to work to. At this initial stage in the design process, information gathering is vitally important. Asking questions of the client (real or hypothetical) will help you in the long run. If you are clear about their requirements at the outset, it saves time making revisions later on.

You need to understand how other designers have tackled similar problems. Books, magazines, museums, galleries, the Internet etc. are all useful sources of information. A work placement with a design studio can be a great advantage, as you will be able to observe how commercial designers approach new projects.

Look at relevant historical examples to boost your knowledge and explore further afield. Different cultures e.g. Japan and America, can have very different approaches, styles and trends.

You also need to look at the production parameters of a project. The size, shape, weight, manufacturing methods and production costs of the final product are all important considerations.

Your brief will determine the size and scale of your work to some extent e.g. you could be asked to produce corporate logos for anything from small packets of food to huge commercial aircraft.

Ergonomics and function are important considerations. A successful product is easy to use and does its intended job efficiently.

Perhaps one of the hardest aspects of graphic design is balancing commercial considerations, the client's vision and the audience's needs with your creative ideas.

▲ Specialist design magazines can be a useful source of information.

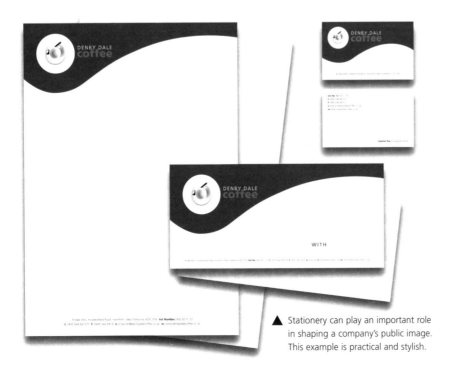

▲ British Airways' logo is instantly recognisable. It appears on everything from marketing material to staff uniforms and aeroplanes.

▲ Stationery can play an important role in shaping a company's public image. This example is practical and stylish.

▲ Experimenting
with an abstract
use of letters.

Methods and Approaches

I think the colour of this leaflet would attract both genders because most men's like these colours and so do most women's but to make sure it is suitable for everyone I will mix in colours together like blue and pink/red. Then I think I will get a better result of people picking up my leaflet.

I think the colour of this leaflet isn't suitable because it only gives attention to women/girls. I think this colour would be suitable if I was aiming for a women/girl to pick it up. To get the colour of this leaflet I used the colour tool in window (paint items). I felt the whole of this leaflet in Adobe Illustrator. I also think men would feel embarrassed to pick up this leaflet.

On this First Design I have Just changed the gradient to Darker colours to see if it would look nice with text and also logo. I think it Looks better with gradients because the colours look more eye-catching, also it isn't easy to see from a far distance. The reason I know that may be seen from far distance is because I have experimented it by going to the end of the class room and it is easy to see to spot it.

On this design I have used light colours because I think it would attract elderly people. The reason I think elderly people would like it, is because they like light, dull colours. It is also calm and not too busy to look at (a lot going on).

▲ Experimenting with different colourways to
find the one with the greatest impact.

To produce the best solutions possible it is important to have a good knowledge of the methods and techniques available to you and to fully understand the requirements of your target audience.

You should already be versed in a range of appropriate techniques, however throughout this course you need to build on them and further develop your knowledge. You should aim to explore as many materials and processes as possible. At the end of the course, your portfolio should demonstrate that you can use a range of techniques and media safely and proficiently.

Not only does this allow you to show off your versatility, it means that when you begin finalising your designs for a particular project you can choose the materials and techniques that are most appropriate for that product and its target audience.

The target audience will have a significant effect on your designs. You need to be clear about their age, income, social background, preferences etc. to produce a successful product that meets their particular needs. This type of information is called demographical data.

Trial and error is an important part of the design process. Don't be afraid to try out different techniques and discard the ones that don't produce satisfactory results. Keep a record of these experiments (either in note form or visual examples), as they will prove to the examiner that you are thinking carefully about your final product.

You can also learn from other designers' successes and mistakes. Look at existing examples of design, both past and present, that relate to your work. Consider how well the product serves its purpose. What aspects of the design work well? What aspects could be improved upon?

Good, accurate drawings should form the foundation for your work in this endorsement. However, with the advancements in technology and computer-aided design, you need to develop sound skills in this area and a good working knowledge of its applications and limitations.

The whole basis of graphic design is the communication of an idea or concept to a third party. With this in mind you will also have to provide evidence of the appropriate use of lettering, signs and symbols as well as images.

Typography is the skilled process of producing printed letters and text. On this course you need to develop a knowledge of the vast and ever-increasing range of letterforms available. You also need to understand their suitability to different design applications e.g. magazine, newspaper, poster or web design, so that you can use them appropriately in your work.

As a graphic designer, you should be interested in the effects, meaning and impact of different forms and styles of lettering.

It is vital that you conduct some research into the history of the printed word and the origins of different typefaces to fully grasp the complexity of this subject. Background knowledge like this will help you to understand the concepts and methodology behind graphic design typography.

You need a good basic knowledge of how a character (i.e. a letter) is constructed and its anatomy (i.e. the names of its component parts). For example, serifs are the small, detailed lines used to finish off the ends of stems, arms and curves in a character. Serifs fall into four categories: Slab, Slab Bracketed, Full Bracketed and Hairline. Characters without these extra strokes are called Sans Serif ('Sans' is French for 'without').

It is generally accepted that serif characters are easier to read and are therefore well suited to large blocks of text (i.e. body text). Sans serif characters are less easy to read, but their clean lines can have a greater impact. Therefore, they are often used for headlines.

Typography

▼ An illustration of the difference between sans serif and serif fonts.
▼ Examples of different typefaces and character sets.

Frutiger (Sans serif) **H** **H** Times (Serif)

Frutiger (Sans serif)
abcdefghijklmnopqrstuvwxyz
ABCDEFGHIJKLMNOPQRSTUVWXYZ

Times (Serif)
abcdefghijklmnopqrstuvwxyz
ABCDEFGHIJKLMNOPQRSTUVWXYZ

When it comes to application, a successful grasp of disposition (i.e. the way in which characters and text are arranged or placed on the page) is essential. This encompasses elements like letter, word and line spacing, orientation, alignment and indentation, all of which contribute to the overall effect and impact a piece of text has on its audience.

Type variations like font size, emboldened text, italics and the use of upper and lower case characters also need considering, as well as the use of colour. You must learn how to mix and match these components and different typefaces effectively. Be careful never to use too many variations in a single piece - this can reduce readability and detract from the message you are trying to convey. Look at existing pieces of typography and experiment with different combinations until you get a feel for what works and what doesn't.

As you can see, typography uses a lot of specialist vocabulary. Make sure you understand the different terms relevant to your work and are comfortable using them.

Information and Communications Technology (ICT) has a range of applications in the field of Art and Design. In particular, advances over recent years have revolutionised the graphic design industry. All the different systems and peripherals available provide amazing scope and work produced within this study area can be just as creative and imaginative as within any of the others.

Used efficiently, computer technology can save both time and money. Repetitive tasks e.g. applying the same formatting to lots of pages, can be automated and you can continually

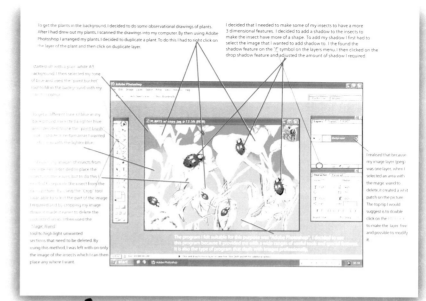

Computer-Aided Design

revise, edit and refine your work without having to start afresh each time. It also has some unique applications. For example, with specialist software you can produce virtual reality images and animated sequences.

Most schools and centres that offer this study option, have various design packages installed on their computers. These might include desktop publishing, printing, drawing, photographic and C.A.D. software. These can all perform a range of different functions. However, it is important to remember that they are just tools and require your instruction and creative input to produce good results.

Desktop publishing software (e.g. QuarkXpress and PageMaker) allows images and graphics imported from devices like scanners and digital cameras to be placed on a page alongside text. You can then move all the different objects around to experiment with alternative designs and create a variety of effects using the different toolbars. This type of software is used in the media industry and is suitable for magazine, leaflet, book and poster design.

C.A.D. software allows you to input coordinates and dimensions and draw lines and arcs to create designs on screen in two and three-dimensions. It can produce complex designs and is often used in product design. Specialist C.A.D. packages are available for different fields, like architecture, engineering, fashion etc.

Regardless of which software package you work with, you must master the different commands and functions and be able to use it competently. You will also need to be familiar with various peripherals, especially common input devices (e.g. digital cameras, scanners and graphics tablets) and output devices (e.g. ink-jet printers, laser printers and plotters).

Your coursework should demonstrate your ability to perform a range of different functions using computer technology. Just as importantly, you need to show that you can choose the right equipment and software for your purpose.

▲ A student annotates a screengrab to show how they used ICT to develop their design.

◄ Digital camera, software packages (Quark Xpress, Freehand, Photoshop), scanner.

Illustration has two main purposes - to explain or decorate text. Sometimes, it does both. Illustrative work is used in a variety of industries, including publishing (books, newspapers, magazines and periodicals), music (album covers and promotional material), advertising, product design and web design.

Consequently, there is a wide range of illustrative styles and genres, from narrative pictures to technical drawings. Different styles require different skills and allow varying degrees of creative freedom. You need to familiarise yourself with as many different styles as possible and understand their specific demands.

You should have no problems finding lots of contemporary examples but remember that contemporary work has been developed for a modern audience and will therefore reflect modern tastes and trends. You will need to look at examples of illustrative work from different periods in time to really understand the scope of this subject and how illustration has developed as an art form.

The starting point for most work within this area tends to be a brief. It is essential that you can define a project by finding out exactly what is required of you before starting work. As well as guidelines for your illustrations, you might also have a budget and deadline to work to, just as a professional illustrator would.

You must be clear about who the target audience for your work is, as they will play an important part in shaping the work you produce. The media and images you use should demonstrate a good understanding of their requirements and mind-set.

It is important that you practise and develop the skills and techniques that professional illustrators use: from fine art techniques to dissections, plans and elevations. On the technical drawing side, an understanding of isometric and orthographic projection is also important. If you equip yourself with as many skills as possible, you will be able to tackle any brief with ease.

Illustration

▲ Examples of
▼ illustrations produced
for children's books.

Manufacturers all want to promote their products and maximise sales. They rely on advertising and packaging to catch the consumer's eye.

Attention to detail is particularly important in this area. Brochures, posters, advertisements, websites, logos, letterheads and packaging all determine a product/company's public image. You will have to think carefully about every aspect of your design (e.g. text, font, colour and images) and what message they convey to a third party. Never underestimate the impact of your choices.

Developing an understanding of what makes a good brand image is essential. Look at current examples of advertising and packaging critically. What message are they trying to convey? How do they do it? Are they successful? Investigate how designers have approached similar projects in the past. As a starting point, think of some of the most famous brands and advertising campaigns, then try to find out how they were developed.

You need to gather as much information as possible about the wants, needs and tastes of your

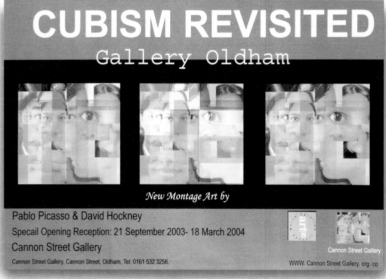

Advertising and Packaging

target audience. This will help you create a design that appeals to them directly, one which they will notice and respond to favourably.

Culture and religion are important considerations. Messages and images that might be appropriate for one social group could be offensive or confusing to another.

If you are producing packaging, form and function are vital considerations. The intended contents will play a significant role in shaping your

designs. The four main objectives to remember are: preserve, protect, inform (or promote) and transport. You will also need to consider more specific requirements. The packaging might have to hold a liquid or a gas and withstand wet conditions or extreme temperatures.

To help you reach a viable solution, you will need to develop the skills needed for producing prototype packaging e.g. drawing nets and modelling with paper and card.

A technical knowledge of a range of packaging materials will allow you to explore lots of possible solutions. Consider the individual properties of each material, the processes involved in using it and the overall cost before making a final selection. Make sure you lead the examiner step-by-step through the selection process, explaining why you discounted some materials and favoured others.

▲ Marketing material for a mobile phone company.
▲ Advertising for a forthcoming exhibition at a local gallery.

As a study area, Printmaking also appears within the Fine Art endorsement (pages 36-45). The distinction is that graphic design work is produced to satisfy a brief, rather than as a free form of expression.

The main print areas you need to familiarise yourself with are Relief Printing (including Letter Press, Lino Printing, Block Printing and Flexography), Intaglio Printing (Gravure), Screen Printing, Planographic Printing (including both Lithography and Offset Lithography) and Dry Printing (including photocopies and laser prints).

All the techniques above have a number of applications. It is vital that you can select the method most appropriate to your work. To do this, an understanding of the different printing techniques is essential and you need to develop good practical skills in as many as possible. Even if your school or college only has the facilities for you to practice one or two different methods, the examiner will still be looking for a good overall knowledge of printmaking.

Factors to consider when selecting appropriate print techniques include quality, quantity and production costs. You can conduct your own

explorations into the surface quality produced by different printing techniques and you might want to try and arrange a visit, or even some work experience, with a local printing works. This will provide you with an invaluable insight into commercial printing practices and give you a better idea of the capabilities and limitations of different techniques.

Artistic flair is just as important as technical ability. You will have to compose items for print, bringing together text, colour and images in your designs to meet the criteria of your brief. One of the greatest challenges of this study area is translating your creative ideas into print.

Studying the work of other printmakers (both past and present) will help you to improve and develop your own work. Look at how individuals approached different projects and realised their ideas in print. It is also a good idea to investigate how the technological advances and art movements of that period influenced their work. Be critical in your studies. If you can identify where others have succeeded, you can apply similar ideas and techniques to your own work.

▶ A traditional copper plate etching press (*top*) and relief press (*bottom*).
▼ A relief print produced using card and a design adapted from a photographic image.

Printmaking

Textiles

Introduction to Textiles

The Textiles endorsement is about producing textiles (e.g. using techniques such as knitting and weaving) and using textiles in a creative way, whether it be to make something functional or decorative. It involves the in depth study of a wide range of materials, processes and techniques from many different cultural origins.

Textiles is a huge subject area - fabrics and materials have an enormous variety of design applications. In your work, you need to show that you recognise this. Try to look at as many different uses as possible, especially within innovative fields like fashion, home furnishings and fine art.

The Textiles course lends itself to experimentation. There is an incredible assortment of materials that you can work with. The rich spectrum of colours and textures available and the wide range of techniques that can be used offer endless possibilities for expressing yourself.

In addition to working with textiles, you will be expected to use other art materials to illustrate your ideas and develop your designs. Try to balance dry materials like coloured pencils, pastels, chalks, charcoal and collage, with wet ones like inks, dyes, acrylic paint and oil paint for maximum effect.

If you are studying Textiles you need to carefully read the information in this section AND the 'Essential Skills and Learning' section at the front of this book (pages 12-32) to make sure you cover all the requirements for the GCSE Art and Design course.

You will be expected to develop and demonstrate a range of specialist skills and work towards producing a final piece within one or more of the following study areas: Printed and/or Dyed Materials, Domestic Textiles, Constructed and/or Applied Textiles, Fashion and/or Costume. You will find more information about the individual subject areas on pages 60-63.

Form and Function

The 'form' of an object or piece of art is its overall shape or configuration; the way in which the different elements are arranged in relation to each other. Form can be directly affected by the function of the object i.e. how it will be used.

Designers often produce work that appears simple but has been carefully developed to meet a specific purpose. You need to be flexible enough to meet the demands of both form and function in your own work without sacrificing creativity.

To explore the ideas of form and function further, you could look at working examples e.g. visit the costume department of your local theatre to see how the demands of the actors on stage affect the design of the garments that they wear.

Most commercial textile designers work to a design brief and you will be expected to do the same. By researching the specific requirements of the brief and looking at existing examples you should, with practice, be able to identify the essential elements of form and function that will need to be included in your designs.

To fully understand the function of an object and its implications, an important part of your research should be to question the person or organisation that set the original brief. It is also worth approaching professional designers working within your field of interest.

The function of the object will dictate the properties that you look for when choosing an appropriate material for construction e.g. it might need to be machine washable, strong and durable. You could visit suppliers or manufacturers. They will be able to advise you on the suitability of different materials for your purpose.

This is a difficult element, but you can use it to demonstrate your ingenuity and ability to obtain relevant information to the examiner.

▲ You must consider both form and function carefully when developing your final design.

▼ Analysing the form and function of existing products can be a good starting point.

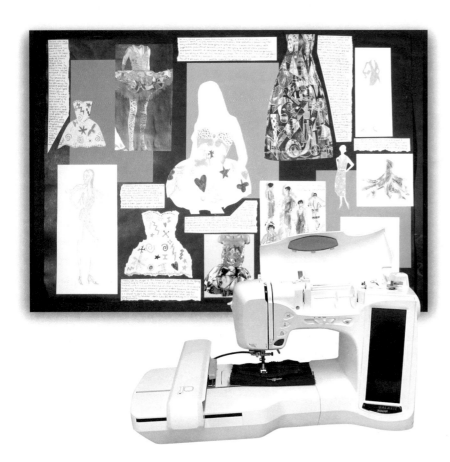

Process and Meaning

Process

It is important that you have a clear understanding of the design process. If you are producing something that is decorative, this can be a fairly fluid process. If you are producing something functional (e.g. a garment), it needs to be more methodical to ensure that the final product meets all the necessary criteria. Both approaches include the same basic steps (see pages 84-101 for more information):

1. **Design Brief / Starting Point**
2. **Preliminary Research**
3. **Generation of Ideas**
4. **Development of Ideas**
5. **Modelling / Finalising Design**
6. **Production of Final Piece**
7. **Evaluation & Analysis**

It is vital that the examiner can trace these steps and clearly follow the design process from start to finish.

Meaning

All pieces of art and design are produced for a reason, whether it is to fulfil a practical function or to communicate an idea. You need to look at existing works and understand the purpose for which they were created. Having done this, you need to ensure that your own work has the same kind of meaning and sense of purpose.

You might want to convey a message using symbolism or produce work that expresses a personal opinion. Refer to the work of other textile artists. You can learn from their work by identifying the methods that they have used to help convey meaning successfully and applying similar methods yourself. If your supporting research and preliminary work is well focused it will help to reinforce the meaning.

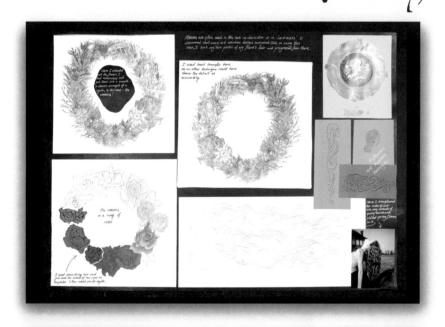

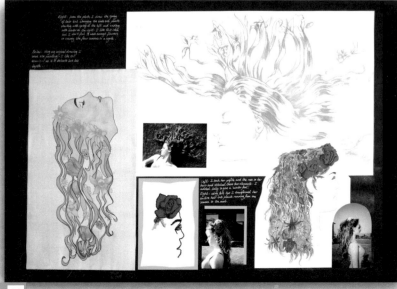

▶ Three mounted boards showing different stages in the design process: preliminary research into the theme of 'seasons', generation of ideas and development of ideas.

Mood

Mood boards are a common device used by designers in the initial stages of the design process. They bring together a whole variety of inspirational materials (e.g. images cut from magazines, pictures and photographs, key words, fabric samples and colour swatches) and can help them decide on an overall 'feel' or theme for a piece of work.

You can use mood boards in your own project, but you must understand their limitations. When developing an idea, they are only useful when combined with sketches, drawings and other preparatory work. Alone, they do not provide enough information to earn you good marks.

Style

Style relates to the overall appearance of a piece. A 'style' is made up of a combination of distinguishing features e.g. the particular way in which colour is applied, shape and form are used and imagery is employed.

Experienced artists and designers often develop their own distinctive styles over time.

Style is also something that can link a lot of different works together within a movement or genre. By conducting some research and deconstructing (i.e. breaking down) these 'styles' you should be able to identify their component parts and the factors that have influenced and inspired them. These factors might include the work of other artists, social or political change or even a manufacturing or production technique.

Mood, Style and Scale

Proportion and Scale

It is important to think about the size of your final product. For pieces of art and domestic textiles, you need to consider the size of the final piece in relation to the size of the room or space for which it is intended. In fashion and costume, size and proportion will be specific to the measurements of the person for whom the garment is intended.

Colour and pattern can be cleverly used to create illusions of size. For example, dark or warm colours and large patterns can make things look smaller, light or cool colours and small patterns can make them look larger.

At the design stage, it is not always possible to produce 'actual' size images. Therefore, the ability to produce scale drawings is an invaluable skill. The size of an object in a scale drawing is directly proportional to the size of the actual object e.g. 1 unit of measurement in the drawing represents 5 units of measurements in 'real life'.

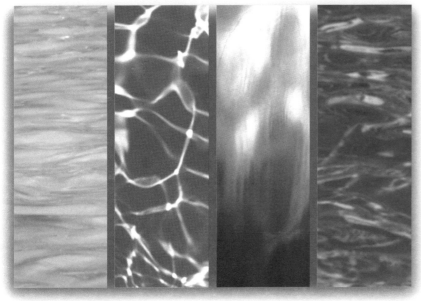

◄ This mood board exploring the theme of 'water' combines magazine cuttings and photographs with some experimental work produced by the student.

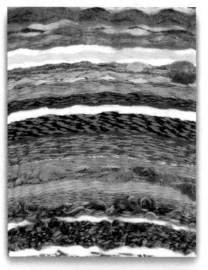
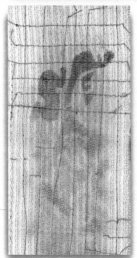

As part of this course, you will need to explore different techniques associated with textile design. Not only will the examiner be looking for evidence that you have done this, it is in your interest too. If you look at as many different methods as possible, you will give yourself far greater scope for creativity when it comes to producing your final piece.

Below are just some of the methods that you could explore. This list is by no means exhaustive. You should discover more when you conduct your research.

Printing
- Block Printing
- Stencilling
- Screen Printing
- Engraved Roller Printing
- Transfer Printing
- Digital Printing

Dyeing
- Pigment Dyeing
- Natural and Vegetable Dyeing
- Batik
- Tie Dye
- Fabric Paints

Construction
- Weaving
- Knitting
- Patchwork
- Embroidery
- Appliqué
- Quilting
- Felting
- Manipulation (e.g. Shibori)
- Embellishment (e.g. Shisha)

A vital part of the Textiles course is to look at how other artists in this field work. Pay particular attention to how they combine different techniques and disciplines and their use of both traditional and contemporary methods, as this will help when you come to produce your own work.

In exploring all these different ways of working, you are looking for the one that helps you to express your ideas most effectively.

Ways of Working

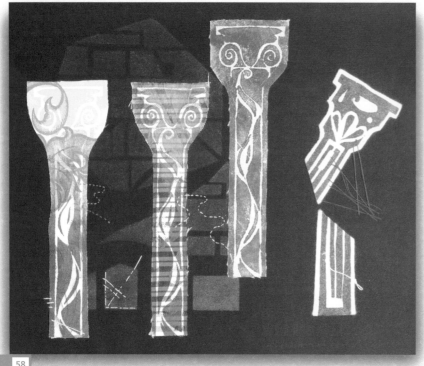

◄ These designs inspired by buildings were produced using different techniques: appliqué, weaving, stencilling, silk painting and relief printing.

Appropriate Methods

The way in which textile artists and designers work can vary greatly, from handicraft to computer-aided technology, depending upon their purpose. Purpose is something you will need to consider carefully when deciding how you will produce your final piece.

To be able to choose methods and processes appropriate to your finished product, you need a good working knowledge of a range of art, craft, design and manufacturing processes.

Based on this knowledge, you should be able to make an accurate assessment of the strengths and weaknesses of each process and recognise where it can be used advantageously and where it is best avoided.

For example, hand-stitching might be appropriate if you are producing a bespoke wall hanging, but it would not be suitable for sewing the seams on a pair of trousers. Machine stitching is much faster and more secure and therefore better suited to this kind of product.

Many contemporary designers use information technology in both the design and the production process. It is essential that you understand some of its applications so that you can make use of them yourself where appropriate. Start by researching some of the C.A.D. (Computer-Aided Design) packages and computerised machinery currently available. If your school or college has any such

equipment, make sure you know how to use it correctly.

The technology and materials used in textile design are potentially hazardous. Machinery can contain fast-moving parts and tools are often sharp. You must be aware of the dangers and be able to adhere to all the appropriate safeguards when using this equipment. (For more information on Safe Working Practices see pages 94-95.)

▲ Explore different methods for producing your final design. This student experimented with techniques like silk-painting, batik and appliqué to find one suitable for her pop art motif.

▶ Silk painting can be used to produce detailed one-off designs. It lends itself to a range of subject matter.

▼ Printing and dyeing methods often require specialist equipment: a batik pot and wax, Tjantings (for applying the wax) and a printing screen.

Printing and Dyeing

Printing

If you choose to study printed materials, it is vital that you research all the different techniques that can be used. You will then need to select one printing method to study in depth and in which to develop technical expertise. You may well find that the specialism of your teacher or lecturer and the facilities at your school or college dictate your choice here.

Printing methods to consider include Mono Printing, Relief Printing, Woodcut or Block Printing, Linocut Printing or Screen-Printing. You can produce simple or complicated designs to great effect depending on which of these techniques you employ.

There is a rich tradition of printed materials throughout history. Your own experimentation may be limited by time, resources and cost, so it is important to explore this heritage to discover just how versatile these techniques can be. Many museums feature examples which you can draw upon.

Traditional hand-printing techniques and styles have a massive influence on today's contemporary designers. In the same way, you should try to develop these traditional techniques for your own purpose, to produce contemporary designs.

Dyeing

Fabric dyeing has a long history. The more traditional techniques, like Batik, Tie-Dyeing and Silk Painting, tend to be popular with students because they are better suited to the classroom than modern industry practices.

Do not think, however, that studying these techniques is an easy option. You must familiarise yourself with the tools and procedures so that you can use them competently. Only once you can do this, will you be able to experiment effectively and discover all the possibilities offered by these methods.

The number of contemporary textile designers who use traditional techniques in a 21st-century context is growing. Looking at examples of their work can help to extend your own knowledge and expertise.

Domestic Textiles

Domestic Textiles are not restricted to soft furnishings e.g. rugs, quilts, cushion covers curtains and table linen. It also incorporates purely decorative pieces such as wall hangings and ornamental objects.

There is a strong historical element to this study area. For centuries, domestic textiles have been produced out of necessity (e.g. blankets and rugs for warmth) and pride (e.g. tapestries and samplers to decorate homes). Consequently, they are an invaluable source of information about social history, providing an insight into the lifestyle of the class, region and period in which they were produced. This means that lots of museums have exhibits relating to the subject.

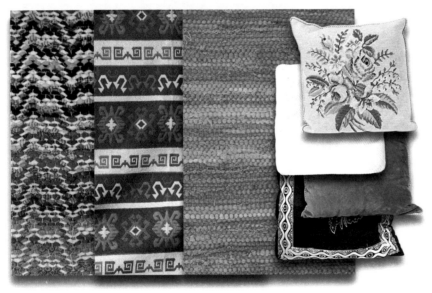

Certain periods can be particularly interesting to study as a background to your own work. For example, the Second World War when rationing and limited resources forced people to be more inventive and ingenious when producing domestic textiles.

Domestic textiles, overlaps with Printed and/or Dyed Textiles and Constructed Textiles. Many of the traditional techniques covered in these study areas, such as hand dyeing, knitting and weaving, have domestic origins. That is to say, they were first practised in the home.

Other traditional methods used to produce domestic textiles include hooking (rugs), quilting, patchwork and tapestry. Try to gain a knowledge of as many of these techniques as possible - it will provide you with more options when you come to produce your own work.

In modern domestic textiles the distinction between practicality and decoration is perhaps less obvious than it has been in the past. Today's consumer often expects products to combine both elements. Therefore, it is important that you can strike a good balance in your work between aesthetics and form and function (see page 55).

This study area covers techniques that can be used to create textiles or develop existing ones. It places a strong emphasis on the surface quality of different cloths and fabrics. You can demonstrate a good understanding of this by using different textures and finishes to create various effects.

You have a lot of freedom on this course and can be very experimental. However, you might want to use the following popular, traditional methods as a starting point:

▶ This decorative piece combines appliqué and embellishment.
▼ Knitting is a highly versatile method of producing textiles.

Construction and Application

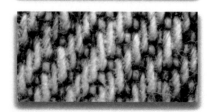

Weaving

Weaving is one of the oldest methods of producing textiles. Try to look at a range of styles and genres from different continents and investigate the different types of loom used for weaving. If you understand how different weaves are produced, you will have lots of options to choose from for creating your own work. You could even develop your own loom.

Knitting

Hand-knitting is the basis of this subject. However, there have been vast developments in knitted textile design in recent years. Knitting machines are becoming more and more complex and the variety of work that they can produce has increased greatly. It is well worth getting to grips with the technology - it will help you to express your ideas far more quickly and efficiently.

Felting

Felt is a thick matt of woollen fibres produced using moisture, heat and vigorous rubbing or applied pressure.

It is an incredibly versatile medium and can be used flat, constructed into sculptural forms or stretched over formers to produce products like hats and shoes. It is used by various ethnic groups to produce clothing, furnishings and tents and by modern industry in the manufacture of everything from pianos to tennis balls. Explore different types of fleece, the properties of the felt they produce and how other fibres (e.g. mohair, cashmere, flax, or alpaca) can be introduced to achieve different qualities.

Other traditional techniques you can draw upon include embroidery, appliqué, patchwork, quilting and Shisha work (a form of embellishment where tiny mirrors are embroidered onto fabrics). Hand techniques like these can be combined with machine technology to produce stunning results.

Some textiles can be manipulated by adding adhesives to give them rigidity or by using heat or chemicals to change their properties. For example, Japanese Shibori involves tying fabric in elaborate patterns and then using heat to 'fix' the design.

This has always been a popular study area. With so many examples to choose from, finding ideas, source materials and fabrics is relatively easy. However, it is important that you only use these for inspiration and work towards producing original designs.

A good fashion designer always produces his or her designs on paper first. Drawing and being able to express yourself on paper is a core part of this study area. Throughout the course you will need to produce sketches, detailed drawings and scale drawings of the final design. It is a good idea to produce a few drawings of models in sample poses that you are happy with, then whenever you want to sketch or develop a garment you can simply trace over one of these poses.

Other specialist skills that you will need to develop for this study area include pattern making and modelling using toiles. A toile is the name given to a prototype garment.

Although many of the clothes seen on the catwalk today are over-elaborate and impractical, most designers produce designs that are suitable for wear. With this in mind, you will need to investigate the actual purpose of fashion. Whatever conclusions you reach should be evident in your work, so that the examiner can see your motivation.

The design process is particularly important in this study area and each stage of development should be reflected in your work. It should be clear how, in finalising your design, you evaluated suitability for use, production methods, materials and patterns. You also need to show the processes used to manufacture the final garment.

Today's designers use a lot of ICT in their production processes and you should look at how it can be used to help you fully develop your own work. The results can be extremely rewarding in terms of both the final piece and the final grade achieved.

▼ A costume inspired by Gaudi's architecture.

Fashion and Costume

3D Design

Introduction to 3D Design

On this course, you will work towards producing a three-dimensional product (i.e. one that has physical length, breadth and depth), which combines functionality and aesthetic qualities. This study area incorporates lots of different disciplines and you can produce work in a variety of media.

As the name suggests, this is a design-led endorsement. You will need to think and work like a designer from the outset. A practical outlook is essential, as is a good understanding of the design process, from brief through research and investigation to final product and

evaluation. You will need to consider the client at all times (whether actual or fictitious), selecting the most suitable solution for your brief and continuing to review and modify your ideas accordingly.

Although your finished product will be three-dimensional, drawing will be an integral part of your work. To save both time and money, designers need to be able to solve problems on paper before transferring their ideas into three dimensions. A sound knowledge of basic concepts like form and function is vital if you are to produce viable solutions.

If you are studying Three-Dimensional Design, you need to carefully read the information in this section AND the 'Essential Skills and Learning' section at the front of this book (pages 12-32) to make sure you cover all the requirements for the GCSE Art and Design course.

You must produce work within one or more of the following study areas: Ceramics, Sculpture, Theatre, Television, Film and/or Exhibition Design, Jewellery and Interior, Product and/or Environmental Design. You will find more information about the individual subject areas on pages 68-72.

Materials and Techniques

▲ Identifying suitable techniques and finishes is an important part of the design process.

▼ This student investigated different slipware techniques to find the one most suitable for her design.

You need a good understanding of a wide variety of materials, tools and techniques relevant to your chosen line of work. Start by learning the theory, and then work towards developing practical skills.

The tools you use on this course will depend upon the resources available at your school or college and the nature of your work. Potentially, however, it could bring you into close contact with some very dangerous equipment.

Kilns, welding and soldering equipment, forges, hearths and foundries, all rely on intense heat, as do the specialist appliances used to manipulate plastics.

Using electrical cutting tools such as drills, saws, lathes, routers, milling machines etc. can help to produce work quickly and efficiently, whilst sanders, planes and grindstones can create a variety of finishes.

It is essential that you know how to use these types of hazardous machinery and equipment correctly and safely. For guidelines and advice on how to do this, turn to pages 94-95.

You must demonstrate to the examiner that you can identify the materials, tools and equipment that are most appropriate to your work. You need to be able to select processes that will help you to produce a good quality product and your research should include technical investigations into different materials to establish whether they are suitable for your purpose. An essential part of the design process is being able to select materials that support and enhance the functions of your final piece.

Throughout the course you should keep a technical notebook. Use this to record step-by-step procedures, recipes for glazes, the properties of different types of timber, finishes that can be applied to metal surfaces… anything that is relevant to your work. You will soon find that this notebook becomes an invaluable reference.

Once you have sketched out some design ideas and explored appropriate materials, you will need to look at methods of construction and plan the most efficient way to build your final piece. The materials that three-dimensional artists work with can often be expensive - careful planning is the best way to avoid costly mistakes and disappointment.

Modelling is one of the best ways of checking to see whether your design ideas are viable. Mock-ups or maquettes made from paper, light-weight card or balsa wood will help you to visualise how a piece will look and should help you to identify any potential problems with

▶ Photograph your final piece at each stage of production.
▼ Producing test pieces is a good way to practise techniques and check the results.

Methods of Working

the design. Working with these inexpensive materials you can refine your design ideas, disassemble the model and make adjustments until you are totally satisfied.

The process of building the model should also help you to work out the construction methods necessary to produce the final piece. If taken apart carefully, the components of a finished scale model can even be used as a pattern or templates.

Models are an excellent way of presenting your ideas to your teacher or lecturer. For some projects e.g. theatre set designs, it might even be appropriate to submit a scale model to the examiner for assessment. Professional stage designers will often present their ideas to the director and stage team in this form so that any potential technical problems or design discrepancies can be dealt with before production begins.

Before you begin construction, make sure you feel confident carrying out all the necessary processes. It is a good idea to produce small, trial pieces to practise and hone your skills before

starting work on the final piece. Make sure you keep all your models and trial pieces; they are an important part of your coursework.

Mistakes and problems are made during construction on even the most carefully planned projects. Don't panic if something does go wrong. If you can demonstrate problem-solving skills and find a practical solution (even if this involves asking someone else for advice) you won't be marked down.

It is a good idea to photograph your final piece at each stage of production. This will help you to lead the examiner through the process step-by-step. It also means that you have a permanent record, should the piece get damaged or broken.

When it comes to assembling your final piece, pay particular attention to detail. The overall finish of the design is the first thing other people will notice, so you don't want to spoil all your hard work with a badly applied glaze or poor paint job. Again, practise different finishes on small trial pieces before applying them to your final design.

You need to think carefully about when and where your final product is going to be used or displayed, as this will influence your design ideas. There are two basic types of setting: interior and exterior. Interiors can range from domestic settings to office or industrial locations and exteriors span both rural and urban landscapes.

Public spaces like shopping malls and community centres can be a good forum for permanent or temporary installations. Alternatively, public parks and gardens can provide opportunities to explore the relationship between design and the landscape. Of course, you will need to obtain permission from the relevant person or committee before you can begin work.

Once you have chosen a site, it is important to examine it closely. Consider how you can make use of its features and visual elements. Remember, when people view your work the setting will influence how they perceive it, so they need to work together to produce a satisfying overall effect.

Depending upon the impression you want to create, you could produce a piece that is sympathetic to its environment or one that creates a strong contrast. Try to anticipate how the public will receive your ideas. You could even conduct a survey to gather opinions.

Your final piece does not have to be static. You could produce a kinetic object that uses wind, water or another power source to create movement. Wind-driven mobiles, water clocks, fountains etc. are all popular public art forms.

Before beginning work on the final piece, you will need to consider the practical implications of your site. For example, if it is an open-air site you will need to use weatherproof

Different Settings

materials. This is an important part of your work and your preparatory studies should clearly show how you have identified and solved any site-related issues.

Think about whether the final piece will be constructed on or off site, how it will be transported (if constructed off site) and how it will be displayed. It must comply with health and safety regulations to ensure that the general public is not put at risk. All installations should be stable, secure and free from sharp edges or hazardous materials. Rather than compromise your creativity, you might be able to find a way around these constraints e.g. by placing the piece out of reach or surrounded by a protective barrier.

A domestic environment can be just as demanding. Try not to overlook small details. Make sure bases are smooth so they do not scratch furniture, teapots pour without dribbling and jewellery doesn't snag on clothes. A little care and attention can make a huge difference to the finished product and your grade.

▲ Look at existing examples of public art and analyse how well suited they are to their settings (*top board*).

◄ The materials, shape and pattern of this bench all reflect its natural setting.

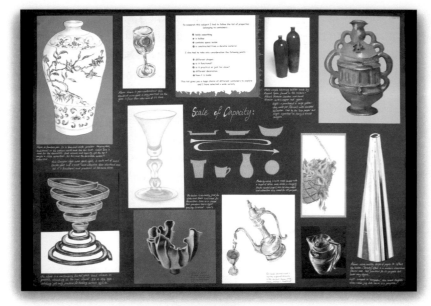

In this study area you will be expected to have a knowledge and understanding of studio ceramics, functional ceramics and ceramics as a sculptural medium, as well as being able to demonstrate the appropriate skills.

There is a wide variety of different techniques associated with ceramic design. They fall into three main categories: casting (including mould making), model making, and jigger-and-jollying or hand-building (including coiling, slab-building and sculpting). In addition, you could try throwing if the facilities are available to you.

You must keep a technical notebook. You need to know how the different processes and techniques associated with firing ceramic work and the differences between biscuit, earthenware and stoneware firings. You should also understand the applications of slips, oxides, colour, glazes and lustre.

There is a long tradition of working with clay. In museums, you will find examples of pottery dating right back to the Neolithic period. The ancient Greeks and Romans were prolific at producing ceramics. Such examples are good to study as they generally combine functional and aesthetic qualities well.

Ceramics

▲ Look at existing examples of ceramic design critically.
▲ These delicate shoes show that ceramic design is not just restricted to vases and bowls.
▼ Pottery from the classical era combines function with aesthetics.

Looking at techniques used by different cultures can be exciting and help you to discover different approaches towards pottery. You could even try experimenting with saggar, pit firings or raku firing.

Make sure you also study the work of contemporary ceramic artists. Look at how they combine traditional techniques with more modern processes and themes. If you think they are effective, it is perfectly acceptable to experiment with similar concepts and techniques in your own work, as long as you do not copy their work and try to pass it off as your own.

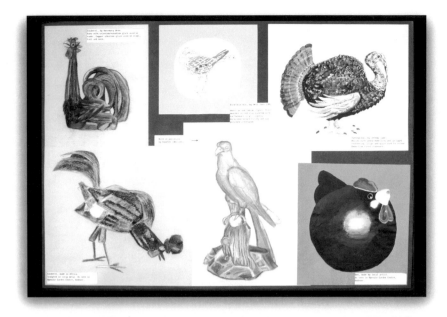

sculpture. Remember that different finishes can affect the properties of a material. For example, clay is porous (it absorbs water), but certain glazes can make it waterproof.

Studying the work of other artists who produce applied art sculpture will benefit your own work. You should be able to find lots of famous examples e.g. Antony Gormley's 'Angel of the North'. Don't just look at the final piece, try to find out what the original brief was and how the artist approached it. Wherever possible, go and view the piece firsthand. This will help you to fully appreciate the relationship between the sculpture and its environment, and the function it fulfils. You should also look at examples from overseas. Temples and churches are a rich source of sculptural applied art.

There are lots of historical periods and art movements, which have produced a plethora of applied art pieces in distinctive styles e.g. the Victorian and Edwardian periods and Art Nouveau, Art Deco and Arts and Crafts Movements. This is an area worth studying as you will hopefully find movements and styles that you find inspirational for your own work.

Sculpture

▲ Studying the work of other designers working to a similar brief can help you develop your own ideas.
▼ A sculptural installation designed specifically for a London Underground Station.

Sculpture also appears in the Fine Art endorsement. To avoid confusion, in Three-Dimensional Design you need to think of it as an applied art form i.e. functional as well as creative. This function might be to fulfil a practical purpose or convey a particular message. Sculptural fountains, commemorative statues and religious effigies are all examples of applied art sculpture.

Your brief might ask you to produce work for a particular location or purpose. If it is a site-specific piece, a significant portion of your work should be dedicated to assessing the site. Visit the intended site, inspect it closely and make a list of all the features that will affect the design of your final piece. For more detailed advice on factors to consider, turn to page 67. Likewise, if the piece has a specific purpose, you need to consider all its implications fully before starting work.

Experimenting with different materials is very important. You will need to look at their properties and decide whether they are suited to the location and function of your

Theatre, Television and Film design involves designing a complete set or series of props for a particular stage or screen production. Alternatively, you could produce work in a specialist field like sound and lighting or costume. Exhibition design entails designing a stand to promote a specific product, suitable for a major exhibition venue.

There are a range of factors that will have to be accounted for in your designs e.g. health and safety considerations, the location of entrances and exits, power supplies, lighting and budget. Site visits are essential to give you a full picture of what you are dealing with.

Because of the potential size of the finished piece, it is acceptable to submit scale models and drawings of the final design for assessment. To accompany your model, you will be expected to produce detailed notes about the construction methods, techniques and materials needed to build the final piece. You will need to develop your technical expertise and produce sample pieces to show that you are proficient in all the necessary skills. Also include swatches and samples of the materials you have chosen.

▶ Rather than design an entire set you may choose to produce a series of props. Masks are a prop frequently used in theatre.

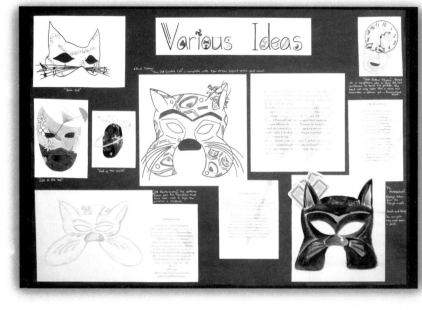

Theatre, Television etc.

Theatrical designers often present their ideas in this form to directors and the production team before embarking on constructing the final piece. It enables adjustments to be made at an early stage and gives both the technical crew and cast an idea of the concepts they will be working with.

You need a good understanding of the roles of the different people involved in this type of design in a commercial environment (e.g. producer, set designer, lighting technician, wardrobe mistress etc.) and a knowledge of how they work together to produce the final piece.

To help you in your work, be sure to look at work produced by other designers and the impact their work

has had on the final production. The choice between a traditional or contemporary approach can make a huge difference to the way in which a play/film is received by different age groups and audiences. It is also worth looking at how a play/film has been advertised. Posters and trailers often reflect a key theme and tie-in with the overall 'feel' of the production.

If you choose this study area, you will need to explore the range of materials and techniques relevant to jewellery making, including those used for forming and embellishing objects made from metals and plastics.

Use a technical notebook to record useful information about different procedures. At the end of the course, your notebook should reflect an understanding of cutting, shaping, bending, soldering, glueing and fastening techniques. You also need to cover some specialist jewellery-making techniques such as casting, wirework and enamelling.

Try to produce samples or test pieces for each technique you look at. Often, the materials jewellers use are expensive, so it is important to practise the necessary skills beforehand. You can also refer back to these test pieces when you need to choose which methods to use for your final piece(s).

Jewellery designers often have to work with extremely sharp tools as well as sources of heat, like soldering irons. You must be aware of the health and safety implications and be able to use such equipment safely. For more information about safe working practices turn to pages 94-95.

Contemporary jewellery designers have a huge range of influences to draw upon. Different cultures have been producing different designs for different purposes for thousands of years. The use of jewellery for adornment, as a status symbol or for ceremonial purposes all make good starting points for a project. Investigating the various styles and techniques used by different cultures or during different periods in history could also help you to come up with good ideas for your own work.

Firsthand study is invaluable. Try to arrange a visit to a local jewellery designer's studio. Watching them work and talking to them about their designs will help to give you a good idea of some of the problems you might encounter in your own work.

Be careful to produce final pieces that are all your own work. You can adapt techniques used by other designers for your own purposes, but your aim is to produce original designs.

▶ Findings, such as earring clasps and brooch pins, are readily available (*images courtesy of Quarto Publishing*).

▼ Metals can be bought in sheet form or as wire, rods or tubes.

▲ Stones, beads and other embellishments can be incorporated into your designs.

Jewellery

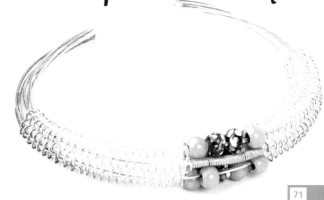

Interior, Product Design etc.

Work in Interior, Product and/or Enviromental Design will almost certainly begin with a brief. Interior design spans both the domestic and working environment, so your final piece could be a design for the home or somewhere like an office, shop or hospital. Environmental design incorporates landscape gardening and spatial design. Product design covers a vast range of possibilities, you might have to redesign an existing product or create something entirely new to perform a specific function.

Projects within this study area can be fairly large scale. In commercial design, such projects involve a whole team of people e.g. the client, project manager, designer, sub-contractors and skilled technicians and craftspeople. As a designer, it is important that you understand what your role would be within such a team.

As a student, it is not practical for you to landscape a park or refurbish a house, so you can submit scale drawings or models for assessment in place of a final piece where appropriate. Even so, it is important that you identify and explore the technical skills that would be involved in actualising your design ideas. You will also need to specify the materials to be used (include samples and swatches wherever possible) e.g. clay, timber, metal, plastic, glass, stone and textiles.

Producing test pieces will help you to compare techniques and finishes and select the ones appropriate for the final piece. Include them in your portfolio to demonstrate your versatility as a designer and show the examiner that you have mastered the necessary skills.

To gain a good understanding of the design process, study how other designers within your field have solved particular problems. Look at how their work developed from design brief to final solution and try to break it down into discrete stages. You can then apply these steps to your own work. Look at the design brief they were given and, if possible, view the resulting designs firsthand. Do you think they have come up with a good solution? What works well and where is there room for improvement? If you can evaluate the work of other designers in this way, you can learn from their successes and failures and improve your own work.

▼ Original ideas generated in response to a brief to design some wall tiles.

▲ This screen is both decorative and functional.

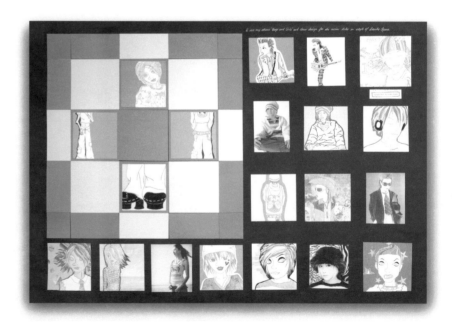

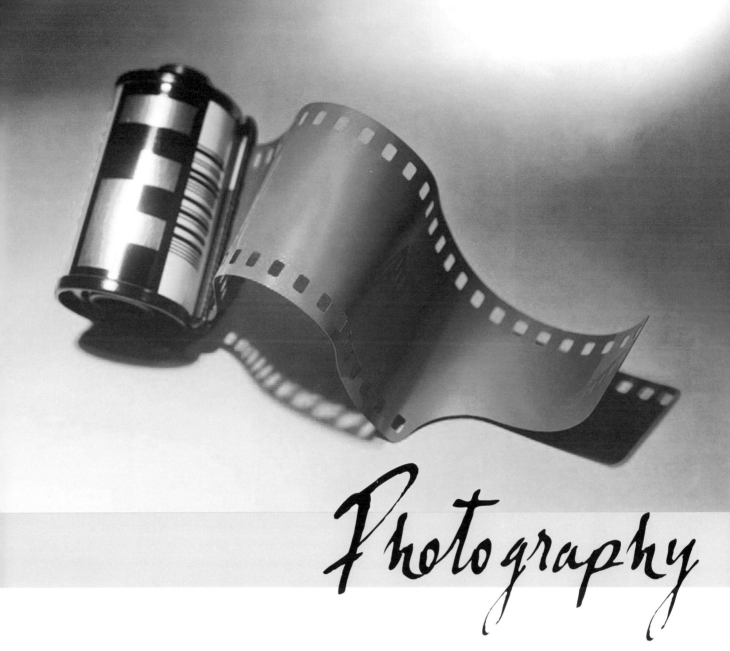

Photography

An Introduction to Photography

On this course, it is important that you move beyond the basic application of photography - simply recording images - and really explore the creative potential of the discipline, combining good technical skills with artistic ability to communicate your ideas and observations.

Start with a good understanding of traditional silver halide photography as most modern digital techniques are based upon the same principles. You can then go on to explore the modern technology available. Some examination boards allow you to use video and film within this endorsement. Check with your teacher/tutor before you undertake any work, though.

Work towards developing an expertise in one specific area. Your choice here may be influenced by the facilities available at your school or college and the specialist skills of your teacher or tutor.

As a background to your work you will need to study the history of photography. You should investigate the relationship between art and photography and how they have changed and developed alongside each other over the years.

Look at examples of both past and contemporary photography. Try to discover the background behind the images so that you can examine them in context. What message do they convey? How does the photographer communicate this message? What does the image say about society at the time it was produced? You can learn a lot about using the different visual elements and composing pictures (see page 22-32) from looking at other artists' work in this way.

If you are studying Photography, you need to carefully read the information in this section AND the 'Essential Skills and Learning' section at the front of this book (pages 12-32) to make sure you cover all the requirements for the GCSE Art and Design course.

You must produce work within one of the following study areas: Portraiture, Documentary and/or Photojournalism, Environmental Photography, Experimental Photography and Working from Objects, Still Life and/or from the Natural World. You will find more information about these individual subject areas on pages 77-80.

▶ A 'good' composition has a pleasing or satisfying feel to it. This is a very personal thing.

Composition

▲ Different viewpoints can have a dramatic effect on the outcome.

Composition refers to the way in which different elements are arranged in relation to each other within an image. It is generally considered that a 'good' composition is one where all the elements are arranged in a harmonious way; to give a pleasing effect.

The difference between an artist and a photographer, is that an artist can choose which elements to show and which not to show, whereas a camera will record everything that the lens sees. However, the photographer can control which elements become the central focus of an image through clever composition, leading the eye to a specific point in the picture.

You need to understand how the camera works to be able to fully control the outcome. Shutter speeds and aperture settings can be adjusted to alter depth of field, light exposure and the way in which movement is captured to achieve different effects e.g. a large aperture gives a short depth of field, so images in the foreground will be in sharp focus, whilst images in the background will be blurred and out of focus.

Different lenses can be used to extend the range of the camera; to record clear images of objects at extremely close range or long range. Wide-angle lenses allow you to photograph a larger horizontal area.

An understanding of how different viewpoints can alter images is also important to composition. Changing the viewpoint might allow you to cut unwanted subject matter from the image, but it can also affect the appearance of the object you are interested in. Experiment by photographing a friend from a high viewpoint, eye-level and a low viewpoint and comparing the images.

It is possible to make some modifications to the composition after the photograph has been taken using different enlargement sizes and cropping techniques.

Regardless of the composition you choose for your final piece, it is always worth including some alternatives in your supporting work along with your contact sheets, to show the examiner that you have considered lots of different approaches. Use annotations to explain your decisions.

To select the best tool for a job, you need a good knowledge of all the options available to you. Start with the basics and familiarise yourself with different types of camera e.g. compact and APS cameras, SLR cameras (single lens reflex cameras), medium and large format cameras, rangefinders and digital cameras.

You need to understand the advantages and disadvantages of each type of camera so you can choose the best one for the type of photography you will be performing.

Explore the different accessories that are available. Tripods and cable releases for remote shutter control can help to eliminate camera shake when slow shutter speeds are being used. Different lenses, filters and flash attachments can all be used in conjunction with the camera to produce different results. You need to identify exactly what you want to achieve and then look to see which accessories can help you to do it.

Once you have a photograph, the image can be manipulated using different equipment in the darkroom during printing e.g. different filters can be used to adjust contrast, burning-in can be used to improve detail and chemicals can be applied to sepia-tone black and white prints.

Use of Equipment

▼ A selection of equipment: tripod, SLR camera, lenses, filters and light.

Experiment with different equipment and keep all the resulting images. You can refer to them to help you make decisions about what equipment and techniques to use for future projects.

A good knowledge of traditional photographic techniques will be an advantage when you move on to look at digital equipment and other modern imaging technology. In manual mode the settings on most digital cameras emulate those of film cameras. Likewise, Adobe Photoshop and similar image-handling software include tools for burning-in, cropping etc. which electronically simulate traditional methods.

If you use a digital camera to produce work, make sure you store all your images for future use. You should also keep an archive or back-up copy of all your images. You can submit CDs or DVDs for assessment, but make sure the images on them are arranged in a way that is easy for the examiner to understand. With key pieces of work it is preferable to make a print using an appropriate printer and good quality paper.

Techniques

Being well versed in different photographic techniques is just as important as being familiar with a wide range of equipment. You need to understand the processes involved and the results achievable using both silver halide and digital techniques.

Practise as many different techniques as possible and include the resulting test pieces in your portfolio to show the examiner how thorough you have been in your work. Keep a note of exactly what you did to achieve each effect so that they can be replicated or improved upon in the future.

Through experimentation you can discover the effects of different film speeds (e.g. 200, 400 and 800 ASA), different types of film (e.g. black and white, colour and slide), different light sources (e.g. natural light, halogen bulbs, spot lighting and flood lighting) and different flash lighting (e.g. built-in flash, flash units and fill-in flash). Again, make sure you keep all the resulting images. They will be an invaluable reference when you are deciding which techniques to use for your final piece and future projects.

It is essential that you develop skills in different darkroom techniques. You should be able to use a range of chemicals safely, observing the need for wet and dry areas in a darkroom set up. You should also know what methods to apply to alter the contrast and composition of an image during printing and how to use burning-in and dodging to control the level of detail.

Through research you should be able to discover other 'tricks' that can be used to manipulate or distort images and achieve different effects e.g. toning, tinting, and solarization.

Digital technology and image-handling software can be very useful when it comes to image manipulation. They speed up the experimentation process dramatically, allowing you to apply different techniques to the same image and save the results under different file names to preserve the original.

Scanners allow you to combine both traditional and modern techniques. An image produced using film can be converted into an electronic file using a scanner. It can then be manipulated using image-handling software.

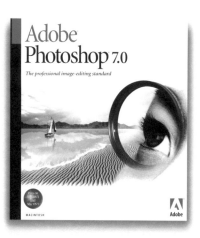

Portraiture

A portrait is a photograph of a person who is aware that they are being photographed. A cooperative model will allow you to experiment with different poses, facial expressions, lighting and even costume.

It is important that you can make the distinction between family 'snaps' and a photographic portrait. A good portrait takes a bit of planning, which often gives it a formal quality that is not apparent in spontaneous 'point and shoot' photographs.

Documentary

Documentary photography focuses on the idea that a picture can tell a story. For example you might try to capture the 'essence' of an event in a single image or use a series of images to record change and development over a period of time. In both cases, it is your ability to communicate meaning through an image that determines whether your work is successful or not.

Photojournalism

There is an obvious overlap between documentary photography and photojournalism, which is about producing images for specific use in the media. Some photojournalists aim to capture a story in an image. However, others produce images to illustrate a key point in a news report or article.

It is important to understand the limitations of these types of photography. Planning is essential - you must be very clear about your aims when you set out and have all the necessary equipment with you. However, more often than not the best photographs are produced as a result of being in the right place at the right time.

Portraiture and Documentary

Both the foreground and background need careful consideration and lighting is particularly important. Shadow and light can be used to achieve desirable effects e.g. highlight or soften different facial features and alter the 'mood' of the photograph.

Explore different viewpoints and positions. Face-on, profile shots and silhouettes all result in very different outcomes. You can also take portraits in different environments. A photograph of the subject in their working environment might bring out a different aspect of their character compared to one taken at home or in a domestic setting.

As an alternative to a single model, you could specialise in group works. These can be very challenging as it takes lots of planning to achieve a successful outcome (i.e. an image where all the subjects are behaving as you would like). You will also need to arrange the group in a way that creates balance and harmony.

▶ The work of Andy Warhol influenced this series of portraits exploring facial expressions.

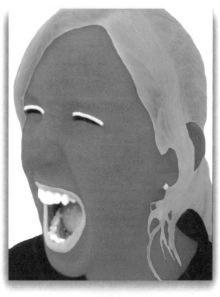

The term 'environment' encompasses interior and exterior environments e.g. the home, work place and natural environment. You might choose to photograph landscapes, buildings and architecture or focus on the smaller details in the world around you. With such a broad subject area, this might seem like an easy option, but it still takes careful planning and patience to produce exciting and original images.

One of the first steps is to choose your subject matter and identify appropriate locations. These will be determined by what you want to achieve in your final piece and what message you want to convey. Even if the environment is not the direct focus of an image, it can play an important role in communicating mood and meaning. For example, a natural environment (e.g. a landscape) can create a dramatically different effect to an urban setting (e.g. a city street scene).

Once you have settled on a location, you should try to visit it several times

▲ A montage of environmental images exploring texture.

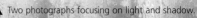

▲ Two photographs focusing on light and shadow.

Environmental

and at different times of the day. You will probably find that the overall feeling of the place is very different in the early morning to the late evening when the quality of light and number of people around changes.

Lighting can be a key factor in creating atmosphere in this type of photography. Try to use the light sources available at your location to maximum effect e.g. moving, coloured lights on a fairground ride, neon signs on a city street or a sunrise over water. You may consider using a flash, but be aware of flooding the subject with too much light or causing a disturbance, especially inside or in a confined

space. Some environments are particularly sensitive to photographers' intrusions. If you want to use such a location make sure you seek permission from the relevant party beforehand.

Other factors to consider include glass, water, mirrors and metallic finishes, which can all reflect light and cause glare or reflect your own image, ruining the photograph.

Make sure you take experimental shots of your location during preliminary visits and try out different viewpoints. Keep a record of the time of day each image is taken, your exposure settings and any other relevant information e.g. weather conditions. These will be an invaluable

reference when it comes to planning a shoot for your final piece.

Because this kind of photography tends to be performed out in the field, it is best to keep your set-up as straight forward as possible. You do not want to have to transport lots of equipment to the site and then spend valuable time setting up complicated arrangements. The best images produced within this area are fairly simple, but show a good understanding of the subject matter. You need to be sympathetic to the environment and produce images that have been carefully composed with special consideration to space and viewpoint.

On this course you are encouraged to move away from producing traditional photographic images and experiment with different equipment and techniques to produce original outcomes. The range of digital equipment, computer technology and modern software available today, used in conjunction with traditional film methods, offers endless possibilities and makes this an exciting and creative field.

There are three main areas to explore within experimental photography:

- the equipment that is used to capture the image
- the way in which the image is recorded
- the way in which the image is printed and processed

In each of these areas it is possible to find alternative approaches to conventional methods. Instead of a standard SLR camera and lens you might decide to experiment with medium format, underwater or panoramic cameras and wide-angle or fish-eye lenses. You could even make your own pinhole camera (camera obscura) or record images directly onto photographic paper (photograms).

Whatever equipment you decide to work with, your first step should be to familiarise yourself with it. Through research, you can find examples of work produced by other photographers using similar resources. This will give you a good idea of what can be achieved and provide a starting point for you to build upon. Take lots of test shots so that you get used to handling and operating the equipment.

The next step is to experiment with different set-ups and conditions. It is a good idea to take lots of pictures of the same subject, varying viewpoint, exposure settings, lighting, depth of field, focus etc. Keep a note of how each image was produced so that you can compare them and refer back to them later.

The darkroom allows plenty of scope for further exploration. You can take a single image and produce a variety of outcomes by applying different techniques. The surface quality of the paper and adjustments to contrast, toning, tinting, baseboard distortions, solarization etc. can all be used to produce different effects.

Digital software can be used in conjunction with scanned images or those recorded with a digital camera. It can be used to correct imperfections and manipulate images in many different ways. It includes tools to sharpen, blur, replicate, combine and distort images. You can also alter colour settings, contrast, tone, orientation and brightness to produce a host of different outcomes. You should work towards producing a series of images linked by a common theme. This might be an original idea or one influenced by a particular style or practitioner e.g. Andy Warhol or Man Ray.

Experimental

▲ Photograms and contact prints produce interesting results.

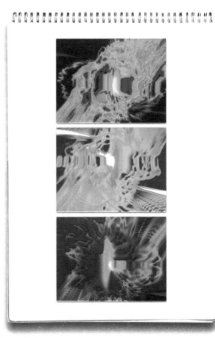

▲ These experimental shots are based around a Sci-Fi theme.

If you are working with Objects, Still Life and/or the Natural World it is often best to keep the techniques you use relatively simple and to focus on the subtleties, using lighting and composition to explore the shape, surface quality and tone of the subject matter.

Whilst your focus will be on the objects, it is important that you do not overlook other factors like background and presentation. An individual object could be photographed in a free-standing position, mounted or placed on a plinth, and still-life compositions need arranging with thought to space, shape and form.

It is worth looking at existing examples of still life in fine art as well as photography. It is interesting to look at how artists approach this

image will look like. You should certainly take lots of test shots to establish the general viewpoint you want to use. On the day of the final shoot you can take a series of photographs varying this viewpoint slightly to ensure you get the image you want. A good tripod will help you to do this.

In the field it is not always possible to take test shots. In this case, make sure you have plenty of film so that you can photograph the same subject using a variety of exposure settings and viewpoints.

Use of colour is an important element in this study area. Black and white photography allows you to focus on texture and tone. However, in the natural world particularly, colour can be used to produce stunning effects.

The 'natural world' also includes wildlife photography. Animals can be both frustrating and rewarding subjects. The best photographs are often the result of being in the right place at the right time. However, careful planning can help. Whether you are photographing a pet in a studio setting, birds in the wild or animals at a zoo, make sure you have plenty of film and all the right equipment with you. Your choice of lens is particularly important. You also need to think about how you are going to cope with movement. You might choose a fast film and shutter speed to help freeze motion or a slower shutter speed to create blurring and give a sense of movement.

▼ As a subject, flowers bring still life and the natural world together.

Objects, Still Life etc.

subject matter; how they compose paintings/drawings and employ the visual elements. You might even try to recreate some art effects using photographic means.

You can also choose to photograph natural objects in their environment e.g. wild flowers. Obviously for this type of photography you will have less control over how the objects are arranged and light sources. You will therefore have to control exposure and composition using shutter speeds, aperture settings, depth of field and viewpoint.

Viewpoint and angles have a significant impact on this type of detailed photography. Just a small adjustment can make a huge difference to the final photograph. Professional photographers often use Polaroid cameras to preview what an

The Unendorsed Course

The endorsed courses featured on the preceding pages (36-80) involve specialising in one specific area of art and design. As an alternative to these you can choose to follow the Unendorsed Course, which allows you to work in more than one of the following areas:

• Fine Art
• Graphic Design
• Textiles
• Three-Dimensional Design
• Photography

At the end of the course, you will submit two, three or four units of coursework for assessment (depending on your exam board). These should encompass two or more of the specialist disciplines.

This is the most popular option in British schools because it offers the most flexibility and creative freedom. It allows you to experiment with a wide variety of materials, techniques and processes, discover new skills and find out which aspects of art and design interest you the most.

Whilst the facilities at your school or college might limit your choices, it is likely that there are several teachers in the art department who all specialise in different disciplines. Together, they will be able to assist you in your work and help you to develop knowledge, skills and understanding in different fields.

Do not think that this is an easy option. The standards for this course are just as high as they are for the endorsed courses. For each unit of coursework you produce, you will need to choose which specialist area you are going to work in and study it in depth.

For each of the specialist areas you choose to study you should turn to the relevant section in this book (see page references below) and read it carefully:

- Fine Art   34-45
- Graphic Design   46-53
- Textiles   54-63
- Three-Dimensional Design   64-72
- Photography   73-80

You are expected to demonstrate all the formal elements and creative skills outlined on these pages. Your work must also address all the assessment objectives covered in the introduction at the beginning of this guide (pages 8-11) and display an understanding of the visual elements (pages 22-32). For advice on structuring your work turn to pages 84-101.

Your background research and study should reflect the range and variety of your practical work. Do not be tempted to recycle information - it will only limit your creativity. Conduct fresh research for each unit of coursework, exploring areas relevant to that particular project and discipline. By the end of the course you should be familiar with the work of practitioners (both past and present) from at least two different fields of art and design and have some knowledge of the history and development of these art forms.

Remember, one of the great advantages of this course is that you will have a broader range of knowledge and skills to draw upon when it comes to the Controlled Test (see pages 102-106).

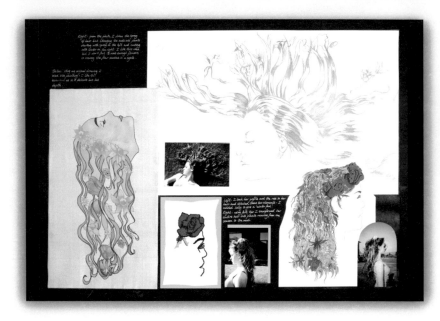

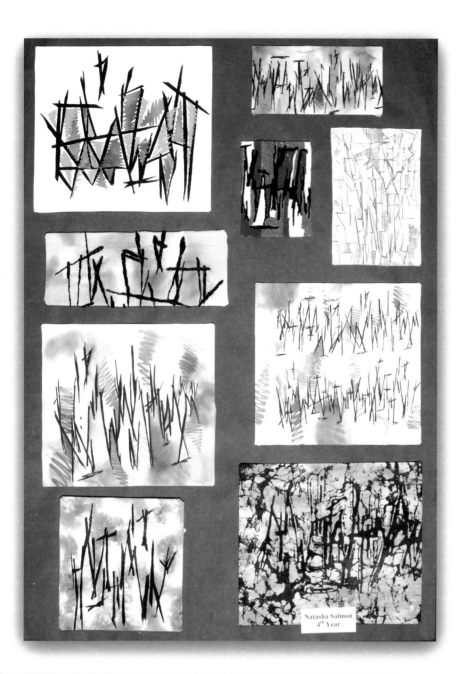

Natasha Salmon
4th Year

◀ These boards, and the screen above, represent three separate units of work produced by one pupil. They show the range and diversity of the unendorsed course.

▼ Photography, ceramics, printmaking and mixed media are just some of the subjects you can explore on this course.

Producing a Unit of Work

Introduction

A unit of work is a 'package' of work produced in response to a single starting point e.g. a theme, brief or idea. It includes all your preparatory work, sketchbooks, logbooks, journals, technical notebooks and the final piece.

Regardless of the endorsement and study area you choose to work in, when it comes to producing a unit of work (for your coursework folder or for the controlled test), it is vital that you follow the same simple steps if

you want to achieve the best results and fulfil all the course requirements.

Art and design is all about communicating your ideas to a third party, in this case the examiner - do it well and you will gain a good final grade. However, if you present a mass of jumbled work with no obvious direction or depth, it doesn't matter how talented you are as an artist, you are not going to impress them.

Your work needs to progress in a

logical manner. The examiner does not know you as a person and has no background knowledge of your work. So, when the unit is presented for assessment (see page 99) it should clearly show how you got from the starting point to your final piece.

The following section looks at the basic framework for a good unit of work. It shows the key stages of development, from starting point to final piece.

When it comes to producing coursework, different schools and colleges have different ways of working. Some will offer their students a selection of set starting points or design briefs to choose from (often taken from old controlled test papers), whilst others will leave it up to the student to find their own direction. On this page is a list of possible starting points for your work:

A Theme

Your work can be based around a common theme e.g. the changing seasons, the four elements, natural forms or festivals.

An Issue

There are many issues - local, regional, national or global - that can trigger ideas e.g. globalisation, drug and alcohol abuse, the greenhouse effect, terrorism or war. Try to choose an issue that you have a genuine interest in - your work will be stronger and more passionate.

Figures

The human form has been a source of inspiration to artists and designers for centuries. You could study specific parts of the body, such as head and torso or hands and feet, alternatively you could focus on movement or the way people interact. You can produce direct, observational work or choose to portray figures in a more abstract way. If you are designing a functional product, you might need to take a more technical approach to the human form and use anthropometric data.

The Environment

Your local environment can provide excellent subject matter, whether it is urban scenes, landscapes or seascapes. You could study elements of perspective, changing light, changing seasons or even weather. You might look at panoramic views or produce close up studies. The way in which artists use space in environmental and landscape design can be a particularly rewarding area of study. You could even look at environmental sculpture and land art.

Critical / Contextual Studies

Exploring why artists, craftspeople and designers produce the work they do can often open up pathways to other areas of study. It also helps to develop a greater knowledge of the world of art. You could study how and why a particular movement came about and then relate this to individual artists or pieces of art within that movement.

Concepts

There might be one aspect of art and design that you find particularly interesting e.g. the way artists represent space or use the abstract. You can make this concept the focus of your investigations, looking at it from a technical viewpoint and with reference to the work of several different artists.

Cultural Studies

Being part of a multicultural society provides an excellent opportunity to study other cultures. Even if you are focusing on just one particular aspect in your work, it is important to try and understand the culture as a whole, including traditions, religious beliefs, moral issues etc. to give your work real depth.

Design Briefs

A design brief will usually provide you with certain key factors that need to be considered e.g. details of the prospective client or target audience, function and cost. It is then up to you to find a practical design solution.

Expression

By studying the way in which other artists communicate emotion in their work, you can learn how to express your own feelings more effectively.

Materials

An in-depth study of a particular material (relevant to your endorsement) e.g. the manufacturing process or its various applications, can generate lots of new ideas.

Still Life

Still life and individual objects have always been an inspiration to artists. It is important that you show a good understanding of the more complex issues behind the aesthetics of a piece. The work you produce could follow a theme, focus on one particular object as a whole or explore the individual characteristics of it.

◀ Mounted boards showing the exploration of different starting points.

▲ A mixed media final piece produced in response to a political issue.

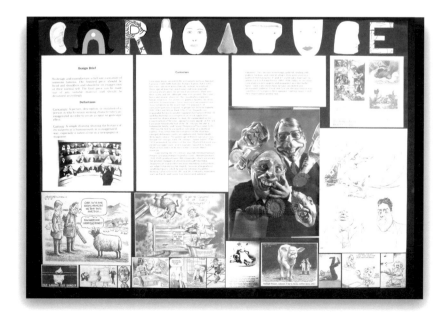

Personal Ideas

The list above is by no means exhaustive and you do not have to use one of these starting points to attain a good mark. You might have an idea noted down in an old sketchbook that you would like to develop, or have stumbled on something interesting when you were investigating a different subject. Before you begin work, talk to your teacher/tutor to make sure your idea is suitable for the course.

The different starting points fall into three main categories: *ideas, themes* and *briefs*.

If you start with an idea, the first step is to put your thoughts down on paper. Then research around your idea to ensure that it is viable. You do not want to start work only to discover, further down the line, that it has no substance. Once you are convinced that your idea will provide enough material to create a strong piece of work, get a second opinion (e.g. from your teacher, lecturer or a practising artist).

If you start with a theme, it can be directly related to art and design or it

Your teacher/tutor might be able to show you examples of work by past students that has achieved high marks. This can be very useful, but you must use it carefully. Ask yourself why the student gained good marks. This is more likely to be attributed to the way in which they worked than their artistic abilities. Use their work as a guide to help you structure your own, but do not copy - you want to produce original work!

Now you need to plan how you will tackle your project. Write down what you want to achieve in this unit of work and how many mounted sheets

you want to produce at the end of it. You now have a starting point and a clear aim, so all you have to do is plan how to get from one to the other.

Break the project down into small, achievable tasks and set yourself a realistic deadline for each one. Your teacher or tutor might even specify these dates for you as part of the initial brief or project outline. It might be hard to be specific at this early stage, but you can still allocate time to research, producing studies, experimentation etc.

Once you have drawn up an action plan, show it to your teacher/tutor to get their approval before proceeding.

Planning

▼ These boards show how students have recorded their initial ideas.

can be something totally random. Again, you will need to conduct some research into the subject. You might find that your initial choice does not offer the depth of inspiration you originally hoped for. Do not be downhearted, your preliminary research might have helped to generate some alternative possibilities.

Most designers, and many artists, use a brief as a starting point for their work. A brief is a set of instructions or a statement that lays out guidelines for a piece. As with the other starting points, the first step is to carry out a bit of background research to make sure you know exactly what is expected of you.

Having conducted some preliminary background research, it is a good idea to do some 'brainstorming' to get your ideas flowing. Your ideas do not need to be complicated; it is often the simple ones that work best.

The next step is to talk to your teacher/tutor. They have your best interests at heart. You can discuss your initial ideas and they can offer you guidance and warn you of any potential pitfalls or avenues to avoid.

Pendant mask
Igdoa, Nigeria
16th Century

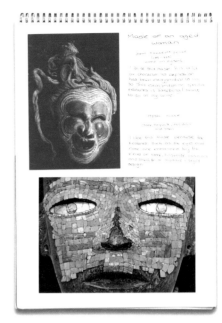

Mask of an aged woman

Keeping Records

For each unit of work, you will need to keep an ongoing record of all your research, ideas, information gathered and work produced. It is best to keep everything together in one place. This allows you to keep track of your thought processes and monitor your progress. It will also be a big help when you need to begin pulling everything together to create the final piece.

You could use a sketchbook, notebook, diary or journal to do this. Choose a format that suits your needs. For example, if you are going to be visiting museums, galleries etc. you will need something easy to carry around. Make sure you submit your sketchbook for assessment at the end of the course. It will show the examiner how you approached the projects and developed your ideas from start to finish.

Notes

As you carry out your research you will need to make lots of notes. Try to keep them as neat as possible - you will need to refer back to them. As well as relevant information about art and artists, keep a step-by-step record of any technical processes that you use in your work. Make sure you write down your ideas, thoughts and feelings as and when they occur to you, whilst they are still fresh in your head.

Photographs

If you have a camera, carry it with you wherever you go - you never know when something interesting or inspiring will catch your eye. Photography is a great way to capture a moment or explore a theme. It is also an excellent way of documenting the various stages in the creation of your final piece e.g. to show a sculpture gradually taking shape.

Images

You need to keep a visual record of the pieces of art, craft and design that you study. At some galleries and museums you can buy postcards of the exhibits. Alternatively, you could take a photograph (always get permission first) or make a sketch.

Artwork

As your work progresses, you will need to try out your ideas and experiment with different materials and techniques. This means you will produce lots of pieces of artwork. Some of these will not fit in your sketchbook or diary. Keep them all together in a portfolio or folder. You might find it helpful to label each item with a number or title. Use this reference number/title if you need to make notes about the piece in your sketchbook - it will make things much easier!

Video

Video and audio tapes can be used to record work of a transitory nature (e.g. a temporary installation) or to capture an event or arts workshop. A clear, easy to follow commentary can help to explain what is going on.

Research

After choosing a starting point and carefully planning your way ahead, you need to begin gathering relevant source materials and carrying out some thorough background research. You should use a good balance of primary and secondary sources to do this.

Try to be methodical in your research. Investigate the resources available at your school or college first: the Internet, library books, magazines, newspapers, periodicals, specialist resources within the art department etc. Information like this, which has been produced by a third party, is 'secondary'.

Having explored the possibilities at your school or college, you will need to venture further afield. An important part of the Art and Design course is to experience pieces of art and design at firsthand. To do this, you can visit museums, galleries, artists' studios etc. Information that you gather firsthand like this is 'primary'.

Although some of the most significant pieces of art are in large collections spread throughout the country, many smaller local galleries have some fine exhibits that are worth seeking out. The advantage of these places is that they are often less busy than their larger counterparts and the curator and gallery staff might be able to spare some time to talk to you.

When visiting a gallery or museum you need to plan ahead. Contact them well ahead of time to confirm opening times and double check that any pieces of art you particularly want to see will definitely be on display when you visit. In some cases you might be able to request to see work from the archives, which is not usually on display to the public. You also need to find out whether you can take photographs of the exhibits or use art materials in the gallery.

Remember to ask if they have a web site. You can use the information online to help prepare for your visit and some galleries and museums even have sites where you can view the exhibits on line.

If you visit an artist's workshop or studio, the same basic rules apply. Plan your trip well in advance and make sure you take everything you need with you. For many artists time is money, so they may only be able to see you once. If you forget to take a spare film or notepad with you, you may well miss your opportunity.

It might be appropriate to visit a design factory to find out about industrial processes. Some of these establishments offer guided tours. Find out if you need to book in advance or visit on a particular day. Ask if they have any resources that you can use. Some places produce information leaflets, worksheets and guidebooks that can help you to build up your background knowledge.

Attending local and national exhibitions of art, design and craftwork can be a rewarding experience. You might discover pieces on show that relate to your own work. Look carefully at the techniques and processes used to create them.

Don't overlook your teacher or tutor as a source of information. He/she is always at hand to give you guidance and can help you to develop and expand your own knowledge and master new skills, techniques and processes.

◀ There are a huge number of museums and galleries all over the UK. Pictured here are the British Museum (London), Design Museum, (London), National Gallery of Scotland (Edinburgh), Bradford Museum of Film and Photography (Bradford), Yorkshire Sculpture Park (Bretton).

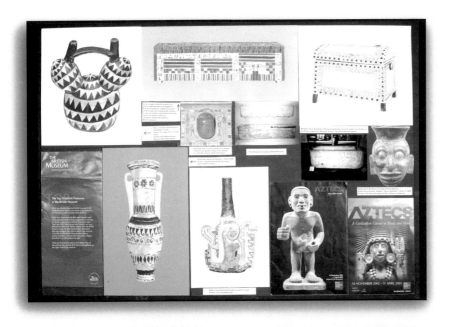

◀ Information gathered during a research trip to London is displayed alongside firsthand studies of some of the exhibits.

▼ Images and notes showing one student's research into how the same subject matter has been treated by different artists and movements throughout history.

There are many other people outside the classroom/studio who can assist you in your work, but it is down to you to search them out. They could include local craftspeople, librarians, gallery owners, arts festival organisers, theatrical agents etc.

These people can offer advice and, used correctly, they can help you to achieve your aims - you just need to ask the right questions. Ask them to look at your work or discuss your ideas with you and note their reaction. These discussions can help to develop existing ideas and generate new ones. They can also highlight aspects of your work that may not have occurred to you before.

This process of gathering information can be extremely profitable. You will begin to discover things that you did not know before and this will help to generate new ideas. The more you learn, the more possibilities you will see for your own work.

Keep your research all together in one place, where you can constantly refer to it e.g. in a folder, portfolio, notebook or sketchbook (see page 89 for more information on keeping records).

You need to produce firsthand studies of paintings, objects and artefacts by other artists. This will help you gain a better understanding of the artistic process and different styles (e.g. abstract and figurative), concepts (e.g. space and perspective) and techniques. You can then apply this knowledge to your own work.

Producing a 'study' is just that. You do not simply copy another artist's work - you explore it and examine it critically.

Start by finding a piece of art that you enjoy or find interesting. First, note down your own feelings about the piece. Why do you like it? What is it that interests you about this particular piece? Try to be as specific as possible.

When you have done this, ask other people if they like it and get them to explain their answer. The more people you ask, the more information you will have to work with.

You then need to find out as much information as possible about the background of the piece. Find out when it was created and why. Who produced it? Is it typical of their work?

Finally, you should look at the piece from a technical viewpoint. How was it created? What processes and materials were used? How has the artist used colour, tone and texture in the piece? When you produce a firsthand study like this, make sure you label it clearly with the artist's name and any other relevant information (e.g. the name of the piece and the date it was produced).

NB. To copy another artist's work and pass it off as your own is against the examination boards' rules and you will be marked down for it. Examiners see numerous units of work each year and many of them are practising teachers and artists in their own right - if you copy someone else's work, it will be spotted.

The next step is to experiment by putting what you have learned into practice. Try producing a few original pieces using the same materials and techniques as the artist you have been studying or by emulating their style. Remember to evaluate the work you produce - do you think the results are successful?

Producing Studies

▼ There are an inconceivable number of artists, designers and crafts people whose work you can study. However, try to look at pieces that will help you develop your own work.

Experimenting

Experimenting with different materials, techniques and processes is an important part of the Art and Design course. Only by comparing lots of different mediums will you be able to choose the one(s) that helps you to express your ideas most effectively.

The type of materials that you use will largely depend on the endorsement you have chosen. However, there are some that are common to all students. Look around your art department / studio and make a list of all the different materials available to you. Set yourself a goal to use all of them in your coursework in some way.

Most departments have a range of paints, different grades of pencil, hard and soft pastels, colour pencils, inks and pens, wax crayons and, perhaps, chalks. You may even be fortunate enough to have printing inks, watercolour pencils, charcoal, graphite sticks and felt-tip pens. Combine any of these with white,

coloured or textured paper and you already have a variety of possibilities to explore.

It is up to you to make the most of the resources available to you. Remember that you are not confined solely to the art department. As well as conventional art supplies, there are lots of potential materials around that are inexpensive and easy to come by (e.g. newspaper, tin foil, natural materials like leaves). Be as inventive and creative as possible. In many cases, persistence and ingenuity can make the difference between a good grade and a mediocre one.

Having identified different materials, you need to experiment with different ways of using them. Your teacher or tutor should be able to advise you on this matter and you can conduct your own research using specialist books, magazines and Internet sites. You can look at other artists' work to help give you different ideas and

extra-curricular art classes at local colleges and centres can be a good way of extending your knowledge. These might be held in the evening, at weekends or, sometimes, during the school holidays. They are usually fairly inexpensive for students to attend and can introduce you to art forms that you do not get a chance to study at school e.g. printmaking, collage, sculpture or batik.

Don't forget to experiment with ICT. Computer-Aided Design (CAD) packages, paint programs and graphics software are all viable tools and present interesting alternatives to more traditional techniques.

Experiment by applying different materials and methods to the same image, design or subject matter to see what works best.
▲ Drawings of birds produced using watercolour pencils on brown wrapping paper and pastels on black sugar paper.
▲ Silk painting and batik are used to reproduce the design.
▲ Using ICT to manipulate a photographic image.

Safe Working Practices

The processes involved in achieving certain effects can bring you into direct contact with hazardous materials and potentially dangerous equipment. You must be able to use them safely to protect yourself and those around you from harm.

Working safely is about using your common sense. On the facing page are some health and safety guidelines that should be observed at all times. This list is by no means comprehensive, and you should ask your teacher or tutor for information about specific regulations put in place by your school or college.

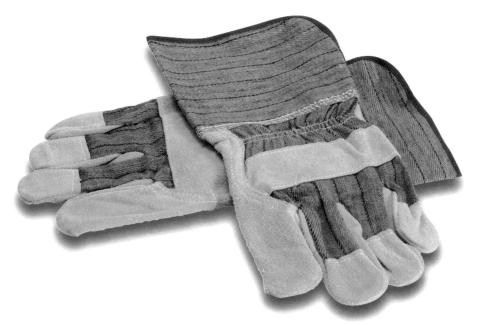

▼ Be aware of signs and stickers that might warn you of potential hazards in the workshop or studio.

General

- Keep the workshop or studio tidy.
- Keep gangways and fire exits clear.
- Clean up spillages immediately.
- Wash and dry your hands properly before and after work using suitable cleansers.
- Always use the protective equipment and clothing provided.
- Use protective gear correctly and make sure it is not worn out or damaged.
- Do not run.
- Make sure you obey all safety signs.
- Take care when lifting heavy objects and use suitable lifting equipment (e.g. trolleys) where appropriate.
- Ensure there is enough heating and lighting to work comfortably.
- Do not smoke in the studio or workshop.
- Make sure you are familiar with evacuation procedures in case of fire.
- Make sure you know where the nearest first-aid point is.
- Report all injuries to your teacher or tutor immediately.

Using Machinery / Equipment

- Keep hair tied back or under a cap.
- Remove any chains or jewellery that could get caught in moving parts.
- Do not wear loose or baggy clothes.
- Never use equipment or machinery unsupervised.
- Always make sure the mains electricity is switched off before connecting or disconnecting equipment or machinery.
- Cables and leads must not be stretched across gangways or left trailing.
- Do not use equipment or machinery unless you know how to operate it correctly.
- Make sure you know where the 'emergency stop' is located.
- Only use equipment and machinery for the purpose for which it is intended.
- Always use the safety guards provided.
- Do not distract others whilst they are using equipment or machinery.
- Never use compressed air to clean machinery.
- All equipment and machinery should be checked and tested for safety at regular intervals.

Knives and Hand Tools

- Only ever use the correct knife or tool for a particular job. If you are unsure, ask.
- Never use worn or broken tools.
- Never misuse tools.
- Clean tools properly after use and store them safely in their correct location.

Hazardous Substances

There are regulations (COSHH) to protect you from hazardous substances used at school or work. Some of the substances are so common, you may not even realise how harmful they can be.

- Read all hazard warnings and instruction labels on containers carefully.
- Always wear gloves, goggles or protective clothing if instructed to do so.
- Before you use a substance, make sure you know what to do if it spills onto clothing or skin.
- Do not transfer substances into unlabelled / mislabelled containers (no matter how small the amount).
- Keep away from sparks and flames.
- Do not mix any substances unless you are sure it is safe to do so.

Using ICT

- Make sure your chair is adjusted correctly (see diagram alongside).
- Use an anti-glare screen in front of the monitor where possible.
- Take regular breaks to rest your eyes and muscles.

Some people develop aches and pains from carrying out the same activity over and over again. You must report any problems with your eyes or any aches or pains in your wrists, arms or neck to your teacher or tutor immediately.

By this stage, you should have lots of ideas for different directions that your work could take. Now you need to proceed to the next stage and decide which of these ideas are viable (i.e. which ones will actually work).

You need to take one idea at a time and work through it until you reach a conclusion (e.g. a potential final piece). If you think it works, put it to one side; if it doesn't, file it away. Do this with each individual idea and at the end of the process you will be able to make an informed decision about which is the best one to use.

Do not discard any ideas completely. They are an important part of the creative process and can be included for the examiner to see. You need to prove that you have not just followed a linear path, but have looked at a number of solutions before selecting just one to work with.

In your research you will have discovered artists and designers whose work influenced you or whose methods are similar to your own. You can use their work as a guide to help you start developing your ideas, but you should find that your own path gradually leads you away from theirs and eventually leaves it far behind. Remember that you want to produce something completely original.

During this development process, every step that you take needs to be noted. You can use visual references (e.g. photographs and sketches) and annotation to chart your progress. Keeping a record like this will show the examiner how you arrived at your final piece. It also allows you to retrace your steps if necessary and ensures that you do not lose sight of the original starting point.

You need to constantly review and modify your work throughout the development process, to make sure you are heading in the right direction and are happy with the results. If you spot any gaps in your work, fill them in now. Do not leave it until the end of the project as you might forget them.

Ask a friend or a member of your family to glance through your work. If they do not understand it, find out why not. Ask them how you can make your work easier to follow and understand and alter it accordingly.

Developing Ideas

▼ This board shows how the student explored and developed one idea for a wall hanging based around the theme of 'changing seasons'.

▲ This board shows the student bringing together all the elements that will make up the final piece (shown alongside).

Finalising Designs

Professional artists, designers and craftspeople spend a lot of time finalising and fine-tuning their designs to ensure that they are completely happy with them, before they begin work on the actual product or final piece. If they are producing work for a gallery or client, they also get feedback from them at this stage to ensure that their design meets all the necessary criteria.

Time is precious and materials are expensive, so it is important that they plan out their final piece thoroughly to avoid costly mistakes and to protect their reputation.

You will also be expected to do this. You have already done all the hard work - conducting research, producing studies, experimenting with materials, etc. - now, with all this information at your fingertips you can sit down and carefully plan the design and production of your final piece.

You will need to produce a full-size or scale drawing of the final piece. This,

in turn, will enable you to produce a list of all the materials and equipment you are going to need and all the processes you will use. You must then make sure that all the necessary items are available to you. Be aware of what could go wrong in the production process and try to plan for all eventualities. Finally, work out how long it will take you to make the piece and calculate how much it will cost.

At this stage, it is vital that you get approval from your teacher or tutor. They may also be able to suggest possible changes to improve your work and cheaper solutions to costly processes.

To help you decide how your final piece will look, you could produce a model, mock-up or maquette. These are often used by artists and designers to help realise their ideas and present them to prospective clients. They allow you to ensure that you are completely happy with the final design before beginning actual production. Any necessary adjustments can then be made without

taking up too much time or costing too much money.

Make sure you keep all the preparatory work, sketches and models that you use to help plan and finalise your design together in one place. These are the pieces of work that you should submit for assessment along with the final piece. They will help you to demonstrate how your final piece relates to the brief or starting point you were given.

The examiner needs to be able to see the path that you have followed and how you have pulled all the different threads of work together to produce your final piece. For information on how to present this work, turn to page 99.

It is possible for things to go wrong in the later stages of your work. However, if you have assembled all your work carefully and planned out your final piece in detail, the examiner will still have all the information needed to assess your work.

The Final Piece

▲ A decorative screen and a mixed media composition: both are examples of final pieces.

▲ Your final piece can be a series of related objects/images, like these ceramic jugs.

Your final piece should be the culmination of all the work you produce for one unit. Use it to demonstrate your knowledge, skills and ability. It can be an individual piece or a group of related pieces.

Do not begin work on your final piece until you have completed all your preparatory work and know exactly what you want to achieve.

Be prepared for every eventuality. In some situations, whilst working on your final piece, you might find that one of the elements just doesn't work and that you have to make changes to accommodate this. For example, the finish you decided to use may not look good on the actual piece or the materials you have chosen to use may be more restrictive than you thought.

If you do have to make changes and alterations during production, make sure you keep a record of them. This ensures that there are not any unexplained leaps from your preparatory work to the final piece. Modification is an important part of the design process. You won't lose marks for making changes and amendments at this stage, as long as you provide good reasons for doing so.

That said, when executing your final piece you should try to adhere to your plans as closely as possible. Ensure you keep to your timetable and complete all your set tasks for the day. If you don't do this, you could end up with an unfinished piece or one that is smaller than you originally intended. If this happens your piece will not reflect your true potential and all your hard work and effort will go to waste.

If you fall behind or things appear to be going 'wrong', speak to your teacher or tutor, who will be able to give you help and advice. Do this as soon as possible - often pieces can be salvaged if problems are caught early enough.

If the piece you are working on is delicate or temporary you will need to record your step-by-step progress. You would also be well advised to photograph ceramic objects before they are fired just in case anything goes wrong.

Allow yourself time to ensure that the final piece is presented to its best advantage e.g. mounting or framing photographs and paintings, washing or stretching textiles objects, placing sculptural work upon a plinth or laminating graphic work. These are vital final stages and could make a significant difference to your final marks.

You need to present your work in a way that is easy to follow. It should clearly show what research you carried out and how your findings influenced your work. Your target audience (i.e. the examiner) must be able to see the route you decided to take and why.

The most popular method of displaying work for assessment is to mount it on large, uniform sheets of thick paper or card. These can be kept clean and flat in a cardboard or plastic portfolio. Related pieces of work e.g. photographs, sketches and small artworks should be grouped together and mounted on a single sheet. The advantage of this method is that it allows you to present a unit of work as a 'complete package'.

Label each mounted sheet individually i.e. Sheet 1, Sheet 2 etc. If there is an accompanying sketchbook, make sure you use dividers or labels to identify the separate units of work.

The most important element of Art and Design is being able to communicate your thoughts, feelings and ideas to a third party. Annotation is one of the best ways of highlighting the key points in your work. This can be particularly useful if you struggled to express your ideas visually. Make sure you label work clearly using arrows or numbers, so that it is obvious which comment

Presenting Coursework

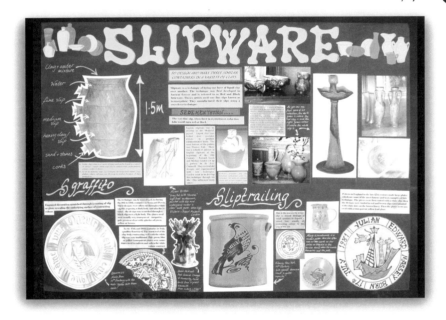

relates to which piece of work. Using ICT can help you to produce notes and annotations that can be clearly understood.

It must be clear to the examiner which of your many studies and pieces of preparatory work have influenced your final piece(s). You cannot display all your preparatory work so select pieces that were significant in the development of your final design.

Make sure your work is colourful and visually exciting. The examiner will see hundreds of units of work, so make sure yours stands out.

You do not have to follow this method of display and may choose another means to present your work. However, it is important to bear in mind that, when you submit work for assessment, the examiner must have the facilities to view it and appreciate its worth. For example, a CD-ROM can be a good way of presenting work where appropriate, providing you divide your work into logical sections so that it is easy to follow.

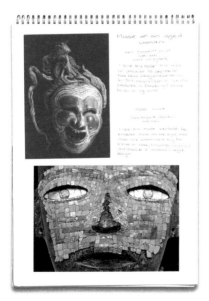

◀ Use notes and annotations to ensure the examiner understands what an image shows and why you have decided to include it.

Evaluating Coursework

You should evaluate your work at regular intervals throughout the course to ensure that it is developing according to plan. You also need to evaluate each unit as a whole once it is complete. The purpose of this final evaluation is to sum up what you have learned.

Start by looking at the information you gathered. Where did it come from and how did it help you?

Look back at the artists and artwork that first inspired you. What did you learn from them? How does your work compare to theirs? Have your perceptions and opinions of them changed as a result of your own work?

Review all the materials and techniques you used. How did you use them? Did you encounter any problems? What do you think of the results?

Then look at your final piece. What do you like and dislike about the piece? Does it achieve what you set out to do? What would you like to change about it if you had more time? Try to be as honest as possible and make sure that your comments are constructive. Always back them up with valid reasons.

Finish by looking at the unit of work as a whole. Did you achieve all your original aims? If you had to repeat the project, what would you do differently? You could also write down any ideas that this work generated, which you would like to develop further given the chance.

▲ Submit an honest evaluation for assessment alongside a photograph or image of the final piece.

At the end of the course, you will need to submit all your work (your coursework units and the work you produced for the controlled test) for assessment. It will be marked by your art teacher or tutor first and then by an external examiner.

Because of the sheer volume of work being submitted for assessment, it is vital that you label all your pieces clearly. It doesn't matter how you do this, the important thing is that each mounted sheet, sketchbook etc. has the following information on the back:

- Your full name
- Your candidate number
- Your centre name
- Your centre number
- The syllabus code for that particular unit
- The date of the examination (work for the controlled test)

You will also need to sign a candidate record form, which is then countersigned by your course teacher or tutor. This form is very important. By signing it, you are confirming that the work you are submitting for assessment is all your own work and not that of someone else. If you had help with your work, you must write down who helped you and why. You are allowed assistance with some machine processes and new techniques, but passing other people's work off as your own is cheating and will not be tolerated.

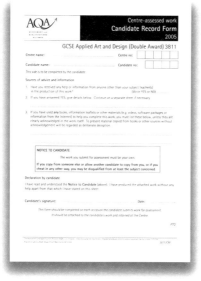

▶ You will have to complete and sign a candidate record or authentication form to confirm the work submitted is your own.

▼ Some exam boards supply labels, which must be attached to each mounted sheet/sketchbook.

Submitting Work

The Controlled Test

The controlled test is perhaps the most daunting part of the Art and Design course. However, as long as you approach it in a logical manner, you shouldn't have any problems.

You are allowed a certain amount of time to prepare for the controlled test e.g. conduct research, experiment with different materials, produce preliminary sketches. This will be 4 or 8 weeks depending upon your examination board. You will be given the set paper at the beginning of this fixed period by your teacher/tutor. A separate paper is issued for each endorsement and the unendorsed study option.

The first page of the set paper will explain exactly what is required of you. Make sure you read it carefully. Use a coloured pen to highlight key words and phrases and ask your teacher or tutor to explain anything you don't understand.

Different examination boards set different papers for the test, but they all follow a similar format. Some offer a choice of different starting points, whilst others give you a theme to explore. A few boards combine both options.

Whatever form your particular paper takes, you will need to approach it in the same way (see pages 104-106).

On this page are some examples of starting points that students have been asked to respond to in previous controlled tests. They are worded in exactly the same way as on the test papers.

You can find specimen assessment papers on the different examination boards' websites.

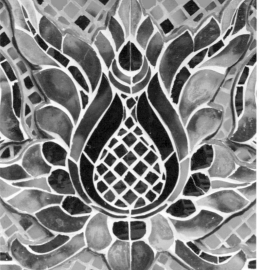

South Asia (AQA)

The arts and crafts of South Asia, including painting, sculpture, architecture, textiles and jewellery, are often rich in colour and decoration.

Carry out appropriate research and produce work based on the theme 'An Explosion of Colour'.

Memories (Edexcel)

A sense of time or place, a moment in history, a personal event or one of national or international significance. All are retained in the memories of the witness and participants. Poems, music, letters, photographs, films, postcards, stamps, coins, flowers, novels, pictures, portraits, mementos, presents.

The following list of artists, designers, craftworkers, cultures and art movements may inspire you as you address the Theme or you may like to discuss alternatives with your teacher:

Stanley Spencer, Paul Nash, Peter Howson, Lucas Samaras, Carlo Maria Mariani, Robert Warrens, Marc Chagall, Michael Clark, Sfiso ka Mkame, Sam Nhlengethwa, Native American Art, Anselm Kiefer, Paula Rego, Susan Hiller, Bert Hardy, Clarence John Laughlin, Frida Khalo, Henry Moore, Graham Sutherland, Anthony Gross, John Singer.

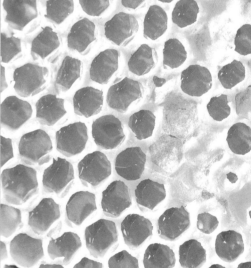

Cubism (AQA)

Picasso, Braque and other artists recorded objects, people and views in exciting ways through a style of working which was named Cubism. Subjects were shown from several viewpoints and artists worked with freedom in the use of composition and colour. Study Cubist works, develop your ideas and produce your own work based on one of the following themes: (a) Dance, (b) Music, (c) Drama.

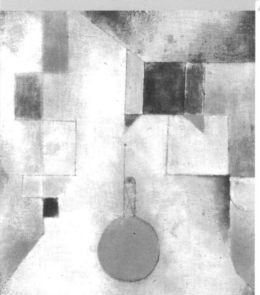

Cell (OCR)

Living cell, growing structure, splitting, dividing, small room as in prison or monastery, small dwelling, grave, cavity, honeycomb, small political organisation, divisions in a plate battery, compartments between the ribs of a vaulted structure, compartments of a box, filigree spaces in precious metal work or enamelling, a group of enclosed units in a tightly meshed pattern, interlocking forms, repetitive shape, tessellation…

As you read through the test paper, ask yourself 'what am I good at?' This is not a good time to take risks with unfamiliar techniques and media. Time is critical, so be realistic about your abilities. Aim to produce something good within the time limit, rather than begin something spectacular that you will not be able to complete.

Ask for advice from your teachers, friends and family to help identify your strengths and weaknesses and then focus on the strong points.

The assessment objectives for the controlled test are the same as those for the coursework (see pages 8-11), so look back at the units of work that you have already produced. Decide which one was the most successful, then identify all the individual elements that went into producing it and apply them to your controlled test.

Make a list of all the different materials, techniques and processes you know how to use competently and aim to utilise them all in your preparatory work or final piece.

Preparation

Remember, this single unit counts for 40% of your final marks and should be the best unit of work you produce. This is your opportunity to show the examiner everything you have achieved in the duration of the course.

▲ Right from the outset, it is clear this student has decided to work with mixed media.
▲ Two boards of preparatory work exploring the theme of 'Conflict'.
◄ Experimenting with words and images.

As you pull all your work together, don't forget to guide the examiner through the development process. Use annotated notes and diagrams to explain every step of the 'journey'. The examiner may not be a specialist in your area of study, so don't be afraid to state the obvious. Ask a family member or friend who doesn't study Art and Design to look through your work. Do they understand it? If not, what can you do to make it clearer?

It is essential that you finish your final piece by the end of the controlled test. You need to demonstrate that you can plan and execute a piece of work effectively in the set time. An unfinished piece shows poor planning.

Write down what you need to do and in what order and then put together a timetable. Be realistic, it is better to allow yourself a bit too much time for each task rather than not enough. Tailor your final piece to the time allowance. This might mean that you have to make your final piece smaller than originally intended, or produce a small section of the piece rather than the entire thing. You must make it clear in your preparatory

▲ These two boards show the student developing some of her ideas.

▲ This sketch of the final piece clearly brings together different elements explored in the preparatory work.

Planning

It is essential that you plan your time carefully, both for the preparatory period (4 or 8 weeks) and the controlled test (10 hours in total). Break the time down into small manageable portions and set yourself realistic targets.

Try to produce a few drawings or pieces of work every day, rather than leave everything until the last minute. It is tremendously satisfying to see your preparatory work gradually build up and you will be amazed how quickly it grows.

You will probably be studying for other examinations at the same time as you are preparing for your controlled test.

Small, daily bursts of energy devoted to Art and Design will often balance and compliment your work in other subjects.

Your preparatory work is not restricted to the classroom; it can be carried out anywhere. Work on it whenever and wherever possible: at home, in the library, during private study time, in museums, galleries, workshops, artists' studios, etc.

At the end of the preparatory period you need to be completely ready for the controlled test. Set aside plenty of time to go over all the work you have produced so far and plan what you need to do during the test.

work that this is what you are going to do and show what the final piece would look like if you had more time.

The examination boards permit you to conduct some processes outside the 10 hour time limit, this includes drying time and kiln firing. Check with your teacher/tutor beforehand if you are unsure and build them into your work schedule.

You will need to allow some time at the end of the exam to draw all the elements of the controlled test unit together and evaluate your work. Refer to page 100 for information on how to do this.

Some schools and colleges will conduct the controlled test (10 hours in total) over two days, whilst others will conduct it over a number of weeks during timetabled lessons.

During the test, you must work under exam conditions i.e. working quietly and with no help from anyone else (including your teacher). You can ask for tools and materials, but all other noise must be kept to a minimum.

Some assistance is permitted when carrying out certain technical processes, like welding and kiln firing.

At the end of a controlled test session, the work produced will be collected in by your teacher or tutor and kept under secure conditions (e.g. in a locked cupboard) to ensure that it is not tampered with. You cannot work on it outside these

The Controlled Test

supervised sessions or take it home with you in the evenings.

Make sure you leave yourself plenty of time towards the end of the test period to get your work in order. At the end of the 10 hour controlled test you must hand in the entire unit of work - all your preparatory work and the final piece - regardless of whether it is finished or not.

▲ The final piece.
◀ At the end of the 10 hour controlled test you must hand in all your work.

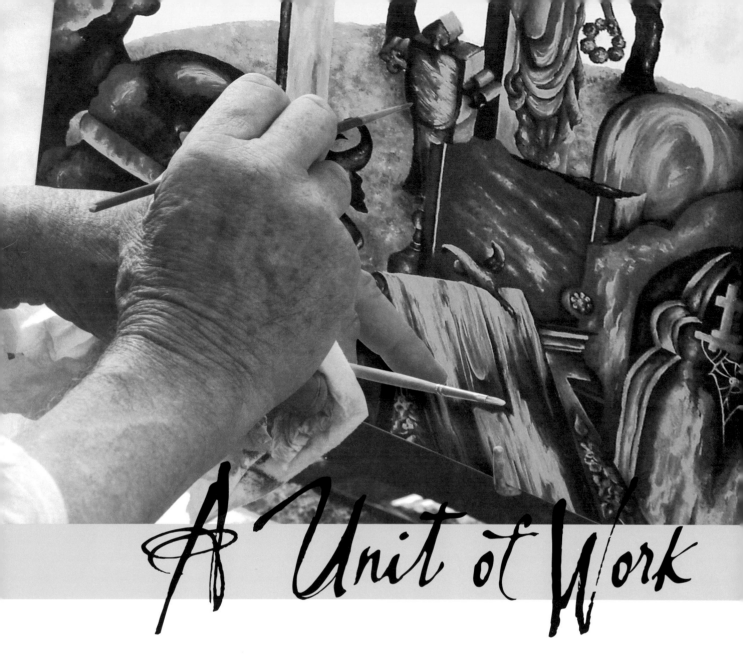

A Unit of Work

The development of an idea is an organic process. It begins with an initial concept and ends with the realisation of that idea in some concrete form. Because this process is so personal, it can be very difficult to make someone else understand how you got from one point to the other.

The separate steps outlined on pages 86-101 will help you structure your coursework in a way that reflects this natural process and communicates your thoughts and intentions at key stages throughout the project. This will help the examiner to follow your progress.

To illustrate how all the steps come together, the following pages show a complete unit of student work. This unit of work encompasses all the assessment objectives of the course

and is presented in a way that clearly shows the development process from start to finish.

Hopefully, you will find these pages a useful reference when it comes to producing and presenting your own work. However, be careful that is all

you use them for. The main criteria of the GCSE Art and Design course is to produce original responses to the starting points you are given. There is no merit in copying the work of other students and you will be penalised if you do so.

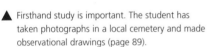

These sketches of gravestones demonstrate excellent *Tonal Skills* (pages 28-29). They portray the relative lightness and darkness of the stonework without resorting to colour.

▼ In this small study you can see how the student has explored the tone further, using chalk on a black background.

▲ Firsthand study is important. The student has taken photographs in a local cemetery and made observational drawings (page 89).

Initial Ideas

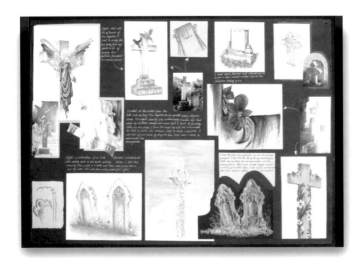

Initially the student produced an in depth study of gravestones and funereal sculpture. This relatively simple subject has been explored and analysed using lots of different materials and techniques, viewpoints and processes. On this sheet the student has explored watercolour, oil pastels, pencil, pen and ink and acrylic paint, showing the examiner that they are capable of working with a variety of different materials (page 16-17).

▲ Here the student has studied how 14th century artist, Fra Angelico painted religious subjects and has experimented with similar techniques (page 92). On the mounted sheets, the accompanying annotation outlines her findings and observations.

▲ The student has looked at celtic patterns from Irish and English crosses circa the 10th century. This historical evidence is based upon *research* done in the school library (pages 90-91).

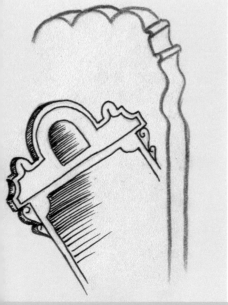

▲ This simple line drawing clearly depicts the *shape* and carving on the gravestone (pages 32-33).

▲ These observational sketches were made in the cemetery. Sketches like these are far more useful than photographs.

Experimenting

On this sheet the student uses images of gargoyles to experiment with different techniques and processes (pages 16-17). Secondary sources like books, magazines and the internet have been used to source these images, which are closely linked to the funereal sculpture on the previous sheet.

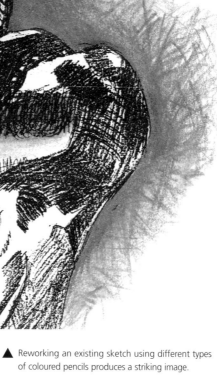

◀ In this painting the student has experimented with *texture* (pages 30-31) and *colour* (pages 24-25) to create a threatening sky behind a silhouetted image.

▲ Reworking an existing sketch using different types of coloured pencils produces a striking image.

▲ Here the student has taken a photograph with a dramatic composition. This image is the inspiration behind some of her paintings.

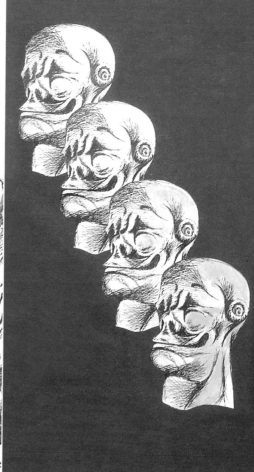

▲ This pencil sketch of a gargoyle shows good use of tone, creating highlights and shadows.

Using photocopies of an existing sketch, the student has added washes of colour and experimented with coloured pencil to create the effect of light falling upon the stone-carved head. ▲

Producing Studies

▼ The student has looked at the treatment of this subject matter by different artists. Here she has taken a painting by Friedrich (*bottom*) and modified it to meet her own needs.

The student has studied the way in which different artists (pages 18-19 and 92) portray ecclesiastical (i.e. relating to the church) subjects, focusing on their use of light and shadow. In the annotation, she has deliberately avoided giving a life history of the artist (which she could have copied from the internet or a book) and discusses why she likes these particular works instead.

▲ Using Monet's series of paintings depicting Rouen Cathedral in
◄ different light as a reference, the student has taken one of her own
gargoyle studies and reproduced it in a similar style (*below left*).

▼ From images of ruined or broken architecture the student
has produced sketches, which begin to explore the structure
of her final composition.

▲ Using Monet's series of paintings of Rouen Cathedral as a guide, the student has used the same composition to experiment with two different colour schemes and maximise the dramatic effect.

Development

This collection of sketches shows the student beginning to develop the composition for her final piece of work. Having experimented with a variety of different approaches, the student starts to consolidate her preparatory pieces. Again, annotations explain her ideas and how she arrived at certain decisions.

My Final Design

▼ A small sketch helps towards finalising the end design. This clearly shows all the different aspects of the preparatorial work being pulled together (page 97).

▲ The sketch of the final design is clearly labelled and all the smaller surrounding sketches relate directly to it. This helps to focus the examiner's attention and reinforce the developmental aspect of the composition.

▼ This sketch shows the student experimenting with pictorial space; arranging the different elements and trying out different compositions.

The Final Piece

In the final piece, the student draws together all the individual elements explored in the preparatory work. She has changed the final design slightly, adapting it to a different, larger paper size.

The use of dramatic colour can be seen throughout the preparatory sheets.

The studies of the gargoyles have been incorporated into the left-hand side of the composition, with the Friedrich style trees in the background. The work the candidate produced on the graveyard can easily be seen.

Glossary

The purpose of this glossary is to provide you with additional information about some of the specialist words and terms that are mentioned in this book.

abstract	art that uses shape, colour and the other visual elements to communicate an idea or feeling rather than portraying something instantly recognisable (the opposite of figurative)
aesthetic	tends to refer to the visual beauty or attractiveness of an image or object
allegory	the use of symbolism to communicate a message or meaning
annotation	explanatory notes
anthropometrics	meaning 'human measurements', this is detailed data about the average measurements of the human form (for males and females at different ages, in different positions etc.) and is often used in product design
aperture	the opening in the lens of a camera that allows light through (normally adjustable)
applied art	art which has a function or purpose but is also aesthetically pleasing
appliqué	a technique used in textiles, where shapes cut from material are attached to a background piece to create an image or design
art movement	a term used to describe a group of artists who all share the same view, idea, style or goal and the work they produce as a result of this
batik	a technique used in textiles, where a design is drawn onto cloth using wax so that when the cloth is dyed these areas remain the original colour
brazing	a soldering technique that uses a mixture of molten brass and zinc to join pieces of metal
burning-in	a technique used during photographic printing, where a selected area of the image is exposed to light for an extended period of time to bring out more detail
chiaroscuro	this means 'light-dark' in Italian and refers to the technique used in painting and drawing, where areas of light and dark are carefully blended to create the illusion of a three-dimensional form
contact sheet	a sheet of thumbnail images (transferred directly from strips of negatives onto photographic paper) used in photography as a visual reference to make image selection easier
cross-hatching	a drawing technique which uses criss-cross lines to shade areas of an image (often used in pen and ink drawings)
decorative art	the name given to examples of applied art that are used for interior decoration purposes
depth of field	used in photography, this is a measurement of the focus range for a particular shot (the total distance over which the subject will be in focus)
dissections	a type of technical drawing, showing the component parts or internal structure of an object
dodging	a technique used during photographic printing, where a selected area of the image is protected from the light source to prevent over exposure
dry point	a printmaking technique, where the design is engraved directly onto a copper plate using a sharp implement
elevation	a two-dimensional, technical drawing of an object from a front or side view that ignores perspective
embellishment	often used in textiles, this means to adorn an object or add something to it e.g. sequins or decorative embroidery, to improve its aesthetic qualities
endorsement	a term used by some exam boards to describe the five course options for GCSE Art & Design, which involve you specialising in a particular subject or discipline
ergonomics	the study of the way in which the human form interacts with its environment, often used in graphic design to ensure a product is easy to use
etching	a form of printing, where the printing plate is made by scratching a design through a layer of protective coating and then using acid to burn it into the metal beneath
figurative	art which portrays or represents something recognisable from the world around you
findings	(when used in jewellery making) refers to basic pre-made clasps, brooch pins, earring backs, ring mounts etc.

Glossary

flexography	a printing technique, which uses flexible rubber/plastic printing plates and quick-drying inks, often used to print on packaging materials and produce repetitive patterns
foundry	a workshop incorporating a furnace, used for casting metals
four-colour process printing	(CMYK) a printing process used by commercial printers, where four colours (cyan, magenta, yellow and black) are laid down in layers to create a single, composite image.
function	the purpose of an object or the job it carries out
galvanize	to protect a metal surface from rust using a zinc coating
genre	a word used instead of 'type' or 'style' to describe different categories of art and design
golden section	(or Golden Mean) a mathematic formula or ratio that was developed to establish the proportions necessary to achieve perfect harmony in a piece of art
gouache	pigment is mixed with gum and water to create an opaque watercolour paint, which has a 'chalky' appearance when dry
Impressionism	a 19th-century French art movement, where the artists' aim was to perfectly capture the quality of light and colour at one particular moment by applying paint in small touches of pure colour
incising	the process of engraving or etching a design into the surface of a base material
Ingres	a type of paper that has a textured surface (and sometimes a watermark), which is often used for pastel and chalk drawings
installation art	a piece of art (often three-dimensional) designed for a specific space or site
Intaglio	a printing technique, where the engraved lines on a metal plate are filled with ink so that the design can then be transferred onto paper
isometric projection	a type of scale drawing used to represent three-dimensional forms on paper (does not take perspective into account)
jigger and jollying	techniques that involve pressing clay against a mould to produce multiple pieces of pottery that are virtually identical in form
kinetic	used to refer to movement e.g. kinetic art is a piece of art that relies on movement to convey a message or achieve its intended purpose
letterpress printing	one of the earliest techniques used in commercial printing, letterpress is a type of relief printing where printing blocks for individual characters (letters or symbols) and words are arranged inside a frame to form sections of text
linocut	a type of block used in relief printing, made by attaching a design cut from a sheet of linoleum onto a wooden base
lithography	a printing technique, where an absorbent material (historically limestone) has a design drawn on it using an oil-based product before being soaked in water. When oil-based ink is then applied, the areas that have absorbed water repel the ink and the areas where the design is drawn attract it, so the design can then be transferred to paper.
low relief construction	a method often associated with collage, where materials are built up to produce an image or design that is raised above the background
lustre	can be applied to ceramics over the top of a glaze to create an iridescent (shimmering) finish
maquette	a small, scale model often used in three-dimensional design to help finalise the design of three-dimensional pieces
media	this is the plural of medium and is used to describe the materials and methods used to produce a piece of art or design
mono print	(or monotype) a printing technique used to produce a single print by drawing the design on the back of a sheet paper, which is laid over an ink-covered surface so that it picks up ink on the reverse side
moral	an understanding of what is accepted to be the right and wrong way of thinking and behaving (by an individual, group, culture or society)

negative space	this refers to any empty space in a painting (or any other art form) that plays an important part in the overall composition
neo-classical	(meaning 'new classical') a style of art, which was first developed in the 16th century, based on Ancient Greek and Roman art and architecture
orthographic projection	a form of technical drawing often used in product design, which shows an object from three separate views: plan, front and side
oxide	a type of chemical used in ceramic glazes to add colour or strength
pacing	a term used in film, usually to describe the rate at which its story or plot unfolds
peripherals	a term used in ICT to describe the devices and pieces of equipment that can be added onto a computer to increase its range of functions e.g. printers and scanners.
perspective	a general term which includes all the different methods used to create the impression of three-dimensions in a two-dimensional (flat) image.
photogram	an image produced by lying objects on photographic paper before exposing it to light, so that after developing they appear as white shapes on a black background
planishing	a process which involves removing bumps and dents from a sheet of metal using a flat-headed hammer
planographic printing	this refers to any method of printing which uses a flat surface (rather than an engraved or relief design) to transfer the design onto paper, material etc. and includes lithography
plan (view)	a type of technical drawing, which shows the object viewed from above and is often used by architects to show the layout of houses
Pop Art	a style of art, which is inspired by different sources from commercial and popular culture e.g. television and billboard advertising, packaging, comic books and pop music
positive space	this refers to the space in paintings (or any other art form) that is taken up by figures and objects
practitioner	a person who works in a particular art, craft or trade (often professionally)
preparatory work	all the work you produce before beginning work on the final piece; generating, developing and fine tuning your ideas.
prototype	a working model (or the first version) of an object or product, used to test if a design idea actually works
raku	a method of producing ceramics that was developed in Japan and involves firing the piece at a low temperature before covering it with a thick glaze
relief printing	a general term used to refer to any printing method where ink is transferred from a raised design onto paper, material etc. (it is important to remember that the final print will be a mirror image of the design on the printing block)
riffler	a double-ended rasp used by sculptors for delicate shaping and smoothing when working with wood, stone, plaster etc.
saggar	a method used in ceramics where the objects are fired within a protective casing
screen printing	this is a printing technique which uses stencils, where the ink or dye is applied evenly by forcing it through a screen made of fine mesh, using a squeegee, onto the paper or cloth below
solarization	(or The Sabattier Effect) a technique used in photographic printing which produces an inverted image (i.e. where black and white are reversed) by re-exposing the image during the development process
spiritual	this is a general term used to describe things that relate to faith, religion and beliefs
symbolism	the use of symbols to represent ideas e.g. a white dove as a symbol of peace
tempera	this is a type of paint, traditionally made by combining a pigment with egg to form an emulsion
toile	a prototype garment made from cheap material so that the design can be altered and modified
viewpoint	the position from which you view something e.g. above or behind

Index